NEW DIRECTIONS FOR PROGRAM EVALUATION
A Publication of the Evaluation Research Society

Secondary Analysis of Available Data Bases

David J. Bowering, *Editor*

Secondary Analysis of Available Data Bases

David J. Bowering, *Editor*

NEW DIRECTIONS FOR PROGRAM EVALUATION
A Publication of the Evaluation Research Society
ERNEST R. HOUSE, *Editor-in-Chief*

Number 22, June 1984

Paperback sourcebooks in
The Jossey-Bass Higher Education and
Social and Behavioral Sciences Series

Jossey-Bass Inc., Publishers
San Francisco • Washington • London

David J. Bowering, (Ed.).
Secondary Analysis of Available Data Bases.
New Directions for Program Evaluation, no. 22.
San Francisco: Jossey-Bass, 1984.

New Directions for Program Evaluation Series
A Publication of the Evaluation Research Society
Ernest R. House, *Editor-in-Chief*

New Directions for Program Evaluation (publication number
USPS 449-050) is published quarterly by Jossey-Bass Inc.,
Publishers, and is sponsored by the Evaluation Research Society.
Second-class postage rates paid at San Francisco, California,
and at additional mailing offices.

Correspondence:
Subscriptions, single-issue orders, change of address notices, undelivered
copies, and other correspondence should be sent to Subscriptions,
Jossey-Bass Inc., Publishers, 433 California Street, San Francisco
California 94104.

Editorial correspondence should be sent to the Editor-in-Chief,
Ernest House, CIRCE-270, Education Building, University of Illinois,
Champaign, Ill. 61820.

Library of Congress Catalogue Card Number LC 83-82735
International Standard Serial Number ISSN 0164-7989
International Standard Book Number ISBN 87589-783-5

Cover art by Willi Baum
Manufactured in the United States of America

Ordering Information

The paperback sourcebooks listed below are published quarterly and can be ordered either by subscription or single-copy.

Subscriptions cost $35.00 per year for institutions, agencies, and libraries. Individuals can subscribe at the special rate of $25.00 per year *if payment is by personal check.* (Note that the full rate of $35.00 applies if payment is by institutional check, even if the subscription is designated for an individual.) Standing orders are accepted. Subscriptions normally begin with the first of the four sourcebooks in the current publication year of the series. When ordering, please indicate if you prefer your subscription to begin with the first issue of the *coming* year.

Single copies are available at $8.95 when payment accompanies order, and *all single-copy orders under $25.00 must include payment.* (California, New Jersey, New York, and Washington, D.C., residents please include appropriate sales tax.) For billed orders, cost per copy is $8.95 plus postage and handling. (Prices subject to change without notice.)

Bulk orders (ten or more copies) of any individual sourcebook are available at the following discounted prices: 10–49 copies, $8.05 each; 50–100 copies, $7.15 each; over 100 copies, *inquire.* Sales tax and postage and handling charges apply as for single copy orders.

To ensure correct and prompt delivery, all orders must give either the *name of an individual* or an *official purchase order number.* Please submit your order as follows:

Subscriptions: specify series and year subscription is to begin.
Single Copies: specify sourcebook code (such as, PE8) and first two words of title.

Mail orders for United States and Possessions, Latin America, Canada, Japan, Australia, and New Zealand to:
Jossey-Bass Inc., Publishers
433 California Street
San Francisco, California 94104

Mail orders for all other parts of the world to:
Jossey-Bass Limited
28 Banner Street
London EC1Y 8QE

New Directions for Program Evaluation Series
Ernest R. House, *Editor-in-Chief*

PE1 *Exploring Purposes and Dimensions,* Scarvia B. Anderson, Claire D. Coles
PE2 *Evaluating Federally Sponsored Programs,* Charlotte C. Rentz, R. Robert Rentz
PE3 *Monitoring Ongoing Programs,* Donald L. Grant
PE4 *Secondary Analysis,* Robert F. Boruch
PE5 *Utilization of Evaluative Information,* Larry A. Braskamp, Robert D. Brown

Contents

Editor's Notes

Perhaps the most costly and time-consuming aspect of evaluation and policy research is the data collection component. Generally speaking, it usually involves a large-scale survey of some kind, and such efforts are invariably outside the resources of the individual researcher and modest research grants. Large data collection efforts consume large amounts of resources — people, time, and money. At the heart of this sourcebook is the proposition that there is an alternative that has been largely overlooked by researchers — the secondary analysis of extant data bases. By the term *data bases*, we mean both data bases in the usual sense of organized data with accompanying software, and data sets which are sometimes simply data files.

There are many large data bases that are regularly and routinely constructed in considerable detail by a variety of government and private agencies. The issues they address vary from demographics on the nation's housing to information on mental health issues in New York state. Some are harder to find than others, but most are available to the public at a surprisingly low cost. Yet, for the most part, they remain unanalyzed.

There are probably a number of reasons for this. Many researchers simply are not aware of their existence; others, who are, shy away from the task of tracking them down; some question the quality of data collected by others, or the validity of adapting data collected for one purpose into a form useful for another. To others, the technical requirements in setting up files, editing them, modifying them, and making them ready for analysis appear to be overwhelming — original data collection is attractive by comparison. Still others are unaware of analytical techniques that will allow them to use extant data bases imaginatively for their own purposes. In the chapters in this sourcebook, the authors have attempted to address these concerns, and to offer those new to secondary analysis advice and guidance in tackling it themselves.

In Chapter One, David E. Myers and Richard C. Rockwell introduce a number of large-scale data bases that are currently available to the public, and provide references that will lead to others. They describe the types of agencies that develop these data and how they can be obtained. Some guidance is given in the detective work of finding a data base, and there is a catalogue of some twenty data bases with information on the source, the variables, and the characteristics of the sample.

In Chapter Two, Jim C. Fortune and Janice K. McBee take the reader through twenty-nine steps that must be taken to set up a file for analysis. They discuss how various characteristics of the data base and its planned use influence the design of the file, and the problems one may expect to encounter. They make the point that all data bases have some noise in them, and that data will vary in quality and precision. They discuss what the researcher must do to learn as much as possible about the data in order to use it and obtain valid results.

In Chapter Three, Loyd D. Andrew has the important message that in order to successfully use a data base the researcher must come to know the data as well as possible, because all may not be what it seems. Andrew describes in detail an existing data base, the Higher Education General Information Survey (HEGIS), to show by example how one might go about this and how the HEGIS data base can and cannot be used because of the nature of the data it contains.

Finally, in Chapter Four, David J. Bowering describes an actual research project in which five years of data from seven separate data bases were used to develop a single integrated data base to address an evaluation question. The integrated data base was subjected to path analysis in order to assess the effects of federal R&D expenditures on the numbers of Ph.D.s conferred at leading research universities. In this study, the resources precluded an extensive field study. Secondary analysis was used, and the choice of analytical approach was influenced by the nature of the extant data bases available.

In summary, this volume introduces the reader to a number of data bases available at relatively low cost, provides some guidance on how to set up files and examine the quality and precision of the data, describes one such data base in detail, and presents a case study in which an evaluation problem was addressed using secondary analysis.

Secondary analysis is not recommended as a panacea for the headaches and costs of original data collection — indeed, secondary analysis has its own problems to contend with. We simply recommend that, before embarking on an expensive data collection effort or abandoning a project because the costs of an original data collection are too extreme, consider secondary analysis of extant data bases as a possible approach. There is some effort involved, but the rewards may well make it worthwhile.

David J. Bowering
Editor

David J. Bowering is vice-president in charge of the Management and Information Sciences Division at Science Management Corporation, Washington, D.C.

*This chapter introduces a variety of data bases that are
compiled at frequent intervals and supplies information
on how to locate and adapt these programs for one's use.*

Large-Scale Data Bases:
Who Produces Them,
How to Obtain Them,
What They Contain

David E. Myers
Richard C. Rockwell

Every year, the federal government conducts more than 200 surveys
and censuses, which require more than five million interviews and
absorb one million hours of respondents' time (Turner and Martin,
1981). The data bases derived from these surveys and censuses are generally made available to researchers at little cost. The U.S. government
maintains the largest survey apparatus in the world, but even more
surveys are conducted every year outside government, ranging from

In this chapter we use the terms *data base, data set,* and *data file* interchangeably
because no consistent differentiation among these terms will be found in the catalogues
and other reference sources to which we refer readers. However, we favor the evolving
usage of *data base* to refer to a more structured form of data set for which a software
system called a *data base management system* provides the researcher a tailored means of
access to the data.

D. J. Bowering (Ed.). *Secondary Analysis of Available Data Bases.* New Directions
for Program Evaluation, no. 22. San Francisco: Jossey-Bass, June 1984.

5

public opinion polls to market surveys. Some of these surveys also produce large-scale data bases that are available at little cost.

These data bases have enormous potential for policy analysis and evaluation research in a wide range of fields. Yet, by and large, they are not used for such purposes. Why do researchers not turn to these sources for their data? Ignorance of their existence is probably the greatest single reason, but the technical and logistical task of locating and using them is a close second. Indeed, the seeming difficulties of this task make original data collection seem to be a more attractive or at least a more feasible alternative. We contend that it need not be so.

This chapter has two aims: first, to acquaint readers with the variety and usefulness of existing data bases; second, to provide policy analysts and evaluation researchers with information that will allow them to locate and make use of the large-scale data bases compiled by the federal government and the major survey research organizations. The data bases on which we focus have several features in common: They are available to the public without restrictions, they are disseminated in a form that can be used on a computer, their samples are large enough that national parameters can be estimated, and they contain data that are useful in policy and evaluation research. Although we emphasize the familiar survey and census, we have also undertaken to alert researchers to data bases generated from records gathered in the administration of federal programs, such as taxation and human service delivery.

This chapter has three sections. The first section reviews the major producing and distributing agencies inside and outside the federal government. It discusses the dissemination of data bases, and it points to additional sources of information on them. The second section shows how to find appropriate data, how to match data with hardware and software, and how to locate necessary expertise, and it discusses costs. The third section provides information on a number of noteworthy data bases, detailing sample sizes and designs, data contents, time periods covered, availability, and contact persons who can help in obtaining the data bases and data sets. It also discusses the issue of compromising an ideal research plan with extant data bases.

The Major Developers of Large-Scale Data Bases

The best-known federal data-collection effort is the decennial Census of Population and Housing, conducted by the U.S. Bureau of the Census. It has three principal strengths for policy researchers: Its sample design yields reliable data for relatively small populations and geographical areas, even for items not collected for every American; its sample size permits estimations for groups that are small fractions of the population, such as the elderly poor or Asian ethnic groups; and its time series is relatively long, with comparable measures dating back to 1950 or earlier in most cases. However, it suffers from two weaknesses: Because the census effort is so enormous, its data are somewhat stale by the time when the data bases are released, and the data are limited in scope, precision, and detail, as would be expected from a brief, general-purpose questionnaire.

More than fifty years ago, the need for better data led the federal government and others both to initiate major sample surveys in addition to the census of population and to inaugurate special-purpose censuses in a variety of fields. The most substantial of these special-purpose censuses is the monthly Current Population Survey, which dates back to 1940. It is the principal source of national information on employment and unemployment in the United States. The 1960s and 1970s saw a surge of interest in the sample survey as a means of observing people and society. During this period, some sixty-four major studies were fielded for the first time. Most have been repeated, and their data can be analyzed as a series of measures that are comparable over time (Taeuber and Rockwell, 1982). Most of these studies are the direct responsibility of federal agencies, which use the data as an integral part of program planning and administration.

The federal government also collects data through a variety of administrative record systems to which virtually every American routinely contributes information. For example, both the Internal Revenue Service and the Social Security Administration have a network of field offices and forms-processing units across the United States. The National Center for Health Statistics uses state health department records to monitor births, illnesses, and deaths, and the Federal Bureau of Investigation issues *Uniform Crime Reports* based on records generated in local police departments. Stock and bond transactions are recorded by the Securities and Exchange Commission. The Department of Agriculture uses applications for benefits to track characteristics of households receiving food stamps. The Department of Defense operates the Defense Manpower Data Center, a large survey program involving chiefly military personnel and their families, and it collects other data from qualifying and placement examinations. The Department of Education's National Center for Education Statistics collects data from administrative records generated in school systems, colleges, and universities. The Department of Labor supports a major national study of labor market experience, and it collects data on job training and placement.

The National Science Foundation conducts surveys of scientists and engineers, and it monitors personnel, equipment, and expenditures on science and technology in government, industry, colleges, and universities. The frequency and timing of these data collections vary, but many are either continuously-operating administrative data collections or annual surveys.

This powerful combination of surveys, censuses, and administrative records provides the policy researcher with continually updated statistical information on diverse aspects of American life. It is the major information resource on which the social sciences learned to draw in their infancy. Indeed, such disciplines as demography and economics were made possible by the numerical data that governments had long collected (Prewitt, 1983). However, despite the many journals and books that already use this information resource, it is apparent to anyone who is familiar with the richness of the data that are available that much more can be mined from these sources. This is particularly true for policy research, which has shown some reluctance to undertake secondary analyses (Hyman, 1972) of extant data bases, with the exception of the decennial census (Bowering, 1982).

Principal Producing Agencies. The Bureau of the Census, which is presently a part of the U.S. Department of Commerce, is the principal survey research organization in the federal government, particularly for demographic and economic subjects. It is probably best known for the decennial Census of Population and Housing, but it conducts a large number of other censuses and periodic surveys. These include the Census of Agriculture; censuses of retail trade, wholesale trade, and service industries; the Census of Construction Industries; the National Housing Survey; the Census of Governments; the Census of Manufacturers; the monthly Current Population Survey with periodic supplements on such topics as adult education, income, employment, and occupational mobility; the Census of Transportation; and the National Crime Survey. Such agencies as the U.S. Department of Agriculture, the U.S. Department of Housing and Urban Development, the Bureau of Labor Statistics of the U.S. Department of Labor, and the Bureau of Justice Statistics of the U.S. Department of Justice contract with the Census Bureau for the collection of data. This contractual arrangement makes it possible to coordinate and standardize sample design, questionnaire format and content, confidentiality protections, and data base design among federal data-collection efforts.

In addition to their contracts with the Census Bureau, the statistical agencies, including the Bureau of Labor Statistics, the Bureau of Justice Statistics, the National Center for Education Statistics, and the

National Center for Health Statistics, collect data through two other modes: First, from time to time, they hire one of the major survey research organizations, such as the Institute for Social Research (ISR), the National Opinion Research Center (NORC), the Research Triangle Institute (RTI), and Westat, to collect data and produce data bases. In some cases, these organizations also analyze the data—an option favored when the data collection requires considerable experimentation and innovation. Attitudinal surveys and panel studies (surveys that repeatedly collect data from the same persons) have created a need for methodological research. The methodology in each area has primarily been developed by social scientists who work in universities and research institutes. However, the Census Bureau has just taken a giant step forward in longitudinal research by initiating its own Survey of Income and Program Participation.

Second, the statistical agencies maintain systems for the collection of data from such organizations as school systems and businesses. For example, the National Center for Education Statistics conducts annual surveys of pupils, personnel, and expenditures in elementary, secondary, and higher education agencies, and the Bureau of Labor Statistics conducts a monthly survey of about 160,000 nonagricultural establishments to obtain data on employment, hours, and earnings.

In addition to the data collected by and on behalf of the federal government, a number of scientifically important surveys are conducted outside the federal government, often with support from private foundations and the National Science Foundation. For example, the NORC conducts the General Social Survey, an omnibus effort to replicate questions that have appeared in national surveys since 1945, and the ISR sponsors the American National Election Studies, biennial surveys of attitudes and behavior related to congressional and presidential elections; it also conducts the Panel Study of Income Dynamics, the first major longitudinal study of changes in the economic well-being of families and individuals.

Principal Academic Disseminating Agencies. The dissemination of data bases is better organized within the academic sector than it is within the federal government. The researcher who wishes to use data collected by one of the academic survey research organizations can start his or her search — and often end it — with the Inter-university Consortium for Political and Social Research (ICPSR). For twenty years, this organization has provided a central repository and dissemination service for machine-readable social science data. Emphasizing data collected by academic researchers, it is a partnership between the Center for Political Studies of the University of Michigan's Institute for Social

Research and more than 230 member universities and colleges. Membership is not a condition for receipt of services. Through linkages with similar organizations based in Europe and with the United Nations, the ICPSR makes a wide range of international cooperative efforts in data utilization possible. Its high standards for data preparation and documentation have set an example for other institutions. There is no comparable central repository in the federal government, although the Machine-Readable Archives Division of the National Archives and Records Service has the potential of serving this function, particularly for data bases of historical interest. For current files, two organizations are important: the Data Users Services Division (DUSD) of the Census Bureau and the National Technical Information Service (NTIS). There are important differences among these organizations. Both the National Archives and the NTIS are passive disseminators of data at the present time; their activity is restricted to reproducing data bases and associated documentation in the form in which they were supplied by the originating agencies. They do not actively attempt to provide expertise on the subject matter of the data bases — a service that the DUSD is well qualified to perform and that it already performs to some extent for data bases collected by the Census Bureau.

The DUSD does have the potential of becoming just as active a disseminator of data bases as the ICPSR by responding aggressively to users' demands for better documentation, more flexible data base design, training, and the development of specialized software. The researcher can expect to deal with knowledgeable persons at the DUSD, although the chronic lack of computer programmers at the Census Bureau can cause long delays. However, the DUSD has not been entirely successful in its role, as evidenced by the emergence of private organizations, such as the National Data Use and Access Laboratories, Inc., that provide services similar to those potential functions of DUSD.

Many specialized statistical agencies have chosen to distribute all or part of their data bases through their own facilities. From the researcher's point of view, this is generally preferable to dissemination through the NTIS, for the reasons indicated above. Several of these "mini-DUSDs" have been innovative in disseminating their data bases, including preparing data bases specifically designed to work with statistical software packages. At least one agency, the Bureau of Justice Statistics, has arranged for the ICPSR to create a special collection of its data, with additional efforts to catalogue and index the data and to train users.

In addition to the ICPSR, there are several other academically based archives. Most specialize in relatively small-sample polls. These archives include the Louis Harris Political Data Center of the University of North Carolina at Chapel Hill, which provides access to the national surveys conducted by the Harris organization; the Roper Center for Public Opinion Research at the University of Connecticut at Storrs, which maintains an international collection of over 10,000 surveys conducted by Roper, Gallup, the newspapers and networks, and other survey organizations; and the NORC, which maintains a library of its own studies. Some of these archives, including the ICPSR, operate under restrictions imposed by the persons or organizations that generated the data bases. For example, under instructions from the original data collectors, the ICPSR can disseminate several data collections only to academic institutions.

Modes of Dissemination. Data may be disseminated in a number of ways, four of which are common today: the magnetic tape file, an important variant of the magnetic tape containing summary statistical records; the extract file, containing only a portion of the data in the entire data base; and the direct linkage of the researcher's computer terminal to the computer hosting the data base. It is also possible and sometimes necessary to contract for analyses to be performed by an organization that holds a monopoly on the data.

The most common form in which the information in data bases is disseminated is magnetic tape containing records of responses of individuals or organizations to survey questions. In almost all cases, the disseminating organization takes steps to protect the privacy of respondents and the confidentiality of responses. This mode of dissemination allows maximum flexibility to the researcher, because it permits the researcher to design tabulations, regressions, and other multivariate analyses more or less as he or she wants them.

The most critical aspect for the researcher of this mode of distribution is not format of the tape itself but rather the quality of the documentation that accompanies it. In the absence of good documentation, an otherwise valuable data set is unusuable for all practical purposes. Documentation tells the researcher what is in the data files and how it is organized and structured, how the data are coded, and how they can be accessed. Before taking any further steps, the potential user must examine the documentation carefully for such surprises as: the use of numeric codes (such as 99) to indicate missing data for one variable and valid data for another; a screen question that totally alters the meaning of an item; a question that did not work, producing unreliable data; and so on. The documentation should include copies of the survey questionnaires, detailed descriptions of the survey sample, a description of the format of machine-readable records on the tape, a list of the numerical codes representing responses, and an account of coding and editing procedures and "marginals" for the basic variables (counts of persons in the sample in the various categories of race, sex, income, education, and so forth). Ideally it also includes "control counts" for all categories of all variables, which enable the researcher to verify the accuracy of his or her data processing against an independent source. (The technical aspects of matching a magnetic tape file with the individual researcher's needs are discussed in the next section of this chapter.)

Another common mode of dissemination is the summary tape — a set of magnetic tapes (often numbering in the hundreds) containing records of tabulations in far greater geographic and subject detail than printed reports on microfiche contain. For example, one set of summary tapes from the 1980 census provides 150 different tables with 1,126 cells of population and housing data for all states, counties, townships or similar units, block groups, enumeration districts, places (including cities, towns, and villages), and congressional districts. Summary tapes have another advantage for the researcher in addition to their great detail: Because the data are in a form that can be manipulated by the computer, it is possible to produce maps, summary charts, and other custom products without having to enter the data into the computer by hand.

When a data base is very large or when it is still being used by a principal investigator, the disseminating organization will often allow the researcher to request only a portion of the data base. Most often this involves specifying the particular variables and portions of the sample in which he or she is interested. This serves to reduce the size of the data base that is disseminated. It may also prevent the researcher from performing certain analyses. Even in the absence of such a require-ment, it is sometimes prudent for the researcher to order an extract or analysis file in order to save processing time, particularly if the data requirements can be spelled out with confidence in advance. However, because research often leads us in directions that we did not anticipate at the outset, most experienced analysts have had the bitter experience of discovering that the analysis file excludes the particular variable that now seems central to the next step in the research. In this case, we must obtain a second analysis file. However, we may still save money and processing time in comparison to working with the full file.

In recent years, it has become possible to connect the researcher's computer terminal directly to the distant computer that "hosts" the data base. This practice eliminates the need for conveying the magnetic tape to the researcher's own installation, adapting it to the computer there, making backup copies to protect against catastrophe, and in some cases designing an analysis file. The host computer often provides software that is particularly well suited to the data base of interest, and there are often knowledgeable personnel at the other end of the telephone line who can provide assistance. The cost of such access varies greatly, depending on the rates charged for the host computer and on surcharges that may be imposed. The calculation of cost is complicated by the fact that most users have to spend a certain amount of computer time putting the data base up on their local computers — a step that can be avoided by using the computer in which the data base is already resident. Most arrangements for on-line access to data bases are at present limited to economic data, but we expect to see them broaden as computing and storage costs decrease and as the use of noneconomic data bases increases. We recommend that researchers should ask the sponsoring agency whether a direct link can be established for the data bases in which they are interested.

In the most restrictive mode of dissemination, the researcher contracts with the personnel at the data base's host computer to perform the analyses. This process is inflexible, because the researcher cannot easily follow clues as they turn up in the data. It is often slow and expensive, and it is subject to misunderstandings that can increase costs and delay the researh. In addition, the researcher is always a step removed from the research, perhaps at some cost to a good understanding of the data base and at some risk of vouching for the accuracy of results derived by persons whom the researcher does not supervise. Despite these disadvantages, there are two reasons why this mode should be considered: First, it can relieve the researcher of having to learn how to use a particular data base that may play a relatively small part in the total research project. Second, it is sometimes the only way in which the researcher can obtain access to data bases that are considered particularly sensitive or where there is unusual potential for the violation of confidentiality. Also, it is to be preferred in cases where the researcher wishes to maintain a proprietary interest. The Bureau of the Census has several data bases for which this is the only means of access.

Locating a Data Base

Sources of Information. Each of the major disseminators of existing data bases publishes a directory of its files. The *Bureau of the Census Catalog* contains abstracts of all products released in recent years, an overview of Census Bureau products, ordering information and forms, and a list of other sources of assistance. This publication is complemented by *A Directory of Federal Statistical Data Files,* which the National Technical Information Service publishes annually. This NTIS directory is naturally broader than the census catalogue; in particular, it is quite useful for the identification of administrative data bases. (It is, however, out of date and should be reissued.) The National Archives publishes the *Catalog of Machine-Readable Records in the National Archives of the United States.* Each of these publications should be in the library of organizations interested in undertaking secondary analyses.

The ICPSR publishes *A Guide to Resources and Services.* Specialized portions of the collection are catalogued in the *CJAIN Bulletin,* the newsletter of the Criminal Justice Archive and Information Network, and in the *NACDA Bulletin,* the newsletter of the National Archive of Computerized Data on Aging. The Louis Harris Political Data Center has published the *Directory of Louis Harris Public Opinion Machine-Readable Data* and the *Sourcebook of Harris National Surveys: Repeated Questions 1963-1976.* The Roper Center has published *A Guide to Roper Center Resources for the Study of American Race Relations* and *Survey Data for Trend Analysis: An Index to Repeated Questions in U.S. National Surveys Held by the Roper Opinion Research Center;* it also publishes a periodical *Data Set News.*

The journal *The Review of Public Data Use* contains many articles of interest to policy researchers undertaking secondary analyses. Articles consider the statistical methodology of social science and economic measurements, their application to research problems, the development and use of software tools, and the technical, legal, and ethical problems associated with data collection, processing, and use. From time to time, this journal has published current listings of publicly available data bases (for example, Taeuber and Rockwell, 1982). It also publishes articles on data retrieval, such as David's (1980) "Access to Data: The Frustration and Utopia of the Researcher."

The Association of Public Data Users is the principal national organization of users of public data, and the Council of Professional Associations on Federal Statistics links the producers of federal statistics with users. The Committee on National Statistics of the National Research Council undertakes inquiries designed to improve federal statistics themselves. The Social Science Research Council sponsors scholarly committees that seek to advance the ability of the social sciences to make good use of statistics from both federal and nonfederal sources. Most professional organizations in the social sciences sponsor a committee on statistics that represents members' interests in communications with federal producers of statistics and that disseminates information from agencies to members.

Recently, the Gale Research Company began publication of a *Surveys, Polls, Censuses, and Forecasts Directory,* which it describes as a guide to statistical studies in the areas of business, social science, education, science, and technology. However, the majority of the studies listed in the directory make data available that is most often in the form of printed reports, maps, and charts.

Informal channels of information are probably more useful. Personal contacts with other researchers in the same field, scans of the empirical journal literature, and conversations with knowledgeable individuals in data repositories and computer centers all provide unique current information on data bases.

One can formalize this information search by conducting a small-scale telephone or mail survey of fellow researchers who specialize in the substantive area. Each can be asked about the availability of particular data bases as well as about other sources of data. One can learn whether colleagues know of relevant data bases and who the contact persons are. One can also learn the names of other researchers who may know of other data bases that one is seeking. This method is particularly useful for finding data bases that have only recently been assembled or that focus on a relatively narrow topic and that are not well known. This method often turns up data that have been collected as part of an evaluation study.

A large proportion of the empirical research literature is based on the secondary analysis of publicly available data bases. Thus, the literature is a useful guide to the data bases that social scientists have used successfully. Citations point the researcher to these data. Unfortunately, citations vary in quality from the near-useless to careful references based on American Library Association cataloguing rules (Dodd, 1982). The whole research enterprise will benefit when researchers adopt standards for the citation of data bases. A model for citations of machine-readable data files (MRDFs) is provided by the Public Archives of Canada (1983), which have summarized the standards adopted by libraries as follows:

Authorship: The person or institution primarily responsible for the intellectual content of the MRDF, such as the principal investigator, the department or agency, the project director.
Title: The full descriptive title of the MRDF, including dates. No acronyms are acceptable as full titles.
Material Designator: The statement *[machine readable data file]* enclosed in square brackets must be given. The material designation is required to indicate that the information is in computerized form.

Statement of Authorship: The indication of the relationship of the work to the person(s) or corporate body named as principal investigator or to other significant parties, such as the department, funding agency, or sponsoring organization.

Edition Statement: The indication of which MRDF is being described. A change in edition occurs if major additions or deletions of the original MRDF are made or if the variables within the files are altered; major reformatting or major changes in the number of observations or logical records; and changes in the programming statements or language.

Producer Statement: The person or corporate body with the financial and/or administrative responsibility for the creation of the MRDF. The statement includes the name of the producer, as well as the place and date of production.

Distributor Statement: The person or organization that has been designated by the author or producer to reproduce copies of the MRDF being cited. The statement includes the place and date of distribution, as well as the name of the distributor (pp. 1–2).

We strongly recommend that policy researchers doing secondary analyses and editors of scientific journals should adopt these standards.

Matching Data Bases with Research Facilities. Once an appropriate data base has been found, the researcher must determine the form in which the data should be extracted. Knowing that the data are stored on magnetic tape is not enough. Typically, the researcher who asks for a tape from an archive or some other repository will be asked to describe the characteristics that the tape must have if it is to be easily used at the researcher's local facility. To answer this question, the researcher must consider two questions: First, what software will be used to process the data? Second, what type of computer is available at a researcher's computing facility? Technical decisions on importing a data base should be made by experienced users and depend on the answers to these questions.

Some of the most popular software packages are BMDP, SPSS, and SAS. While each of these packages can process raw data, it is sometimes possible to obtain system files that can be processed more efficiently than raw data. This reduces the cost to the user. For example, the National Center for Education Statistics allows users of the High School and Beyond data base to obtain either SPSS or SAS system files. System files are usually software-dependent. To use such files, researchers must know what software is available at the local facility. Obtaining the appropriate file will save both money and time; make sure that the system file created from the raw data meets your needs.

Data structures also differ in whether each record (unit of input for the computer) in the data file refers to a single unit of analysis (for example, individuals, organizations, households) or to a variable. The most common form of data structure is the rectangle file, which contains records referring to observations, and columns referring to variables. For files with this structure, there are as many data records as there are observations in a sample or population — that is, if all information for each observation is contained on a single record. Variations occur when multiple records are used to store data for individual observations or when hierarchical files are used as well as when the structure is inverted. Hierarchical files are often found when one processes data on households (for example, Bureau of the Census Public Use Samples). In these files, the number of data records for individual households varies, because the number of persons in each household varies. Special consideration is required when data files of this nature are used with standard software packages, such as SAS or SPSS. This is not to say that the data cannot be processed with these software packages but that specialized programming is required. One alternative to such programming is to use either Fortran or PL/1 to create files that the standard software packages can analyze without further intervention.

In the second most common type of data structure (the inverted file), data records refer to variables, and columns refer to observations for each unit of analysis. To illustrate this structure, let us examine a data file containing information on county expenditures, revenues, and employment rates. If all data can be stored on a single record, each record refers to a specific variable, such as county expenditures, and the columns of the record refer to all the observations of that variable — county expenditures — for each county in the sample. Many statistical packages cannot process inverted files.

Certain technical magnetic tape characteristics pertaining to the particular computer must also be taken into account when putting a data base up at a local facility. (For the purposes of this chapter, we will assume that the data is stored on magnetic tape.) The characteristics of the tape need to be specified when the data are being processed. It is important to obtain a tape with the appropriate characteristics, since converting a tape into one with the proper characteristics can be costly. Six characteristics must be considered: the tape's density, which is measured in bytes; blocksize (BLKSIZE); logical record length

(LRECL); record formal (RECFM); number of tracks; and code—ASCII (American National Standard Code for Information Interchange) or EBCDIC (Extended Binary Coded Data Interchange). How does the user determine the appropriate characteristics? The best suggestion that we can make is that the user should call the local computer center and ask for a consultant to describe the characteristics that a tape from another facility must have in order to be run at the local facility.

Before the researcher obtains and processes a data base, he or she needs to consider the cost of processing the data. Computing costs are difficult to estimate. One method is to ask other researchers who have used the local computer facility how much it cost to analyze their data. If similar procedures (such as regression analyses or recoding of variables) are being run, then simple extrapolations based on the number of observations and variables may provide a crude estimate of computing costs. If an iterative method (such as multinomial logit analyses) is being used to analyze the data, the cost varies with the structure of the data. Another method is to ask a consultant at the local computer center to run a benchmark test with specific computer procedures so that the researcher can extrapolate to specific problems and estimate computing costs. Researchers should be forewarned that the computing costs are difficult to estimate. Some researchers jokingly advise that the best way of estimating actual costs is to multiply one's best guess by two.

How can costs be reduced? Costs are usually a function of either the number of inputs (I/Os) encountered in processing a data file or of the number of seconds used by the computer's central processing unit. It is critical to know which of these determines the cost of running a computer program. In many cases, particular software packages allow the researcher to reduce the number of I/Os by placing all the data in the computer's core memory; this reduces the number of times that the computer must pass data back and forth between core and storage. The researcher should check with a consultant when trying to determine the most efficient method. As a final suggestion, when many regression analyses are being conducted on the same set of variables, the researcher should use a matrix of moments (sums of cross-products), not the raw data, because the moments need to be calculated once from the raw data file. (Most statistical packages can provide this matrix as an option.) This procedure can reduce costs and time.

A Catalogue of Data Bases

In Table 1, we list some of the major data bases and some of their characteristics. A complete list of extant data bases lies beyond the scope of this chapter. Descriptions of other data bases are documented in

Table 1. Selected Large-Scale Data Bases

Title	Contact	Output	Sample Characteristics	Cycles	Key Variables
American Freshman Survey	Cooperative Institutional Research Program	Published Reports	Annual data since 1966. 1979 survey included data on 190,151 freshmen.	Annual survey since 1966.	Education, Occupation
Annual Housing Survey	Customer Services Branch, Data User Services Division, Bureau of the Census, Washington, D.C. 20233	Micro data file available for each survey. Longitudinal file available for 1974-76 for those housing units in the sample all three years.	Multistage probability sample with over 70,000 housing units.	Annual survey began in 1973.	Housing and Neighborhood Characteristics
Area Resources File	Division of Health Professions Analysis, Bureau of Health Professions, Health Resources Administration, Hyattsville, MD 20782	Summary data file available.	Information in summary form beginning in 1940 for each county in medical personnel, services, etc.	Data beginning in 1940 is updated quarterly.	Health, Expenditures
Census of Population and Housing	Customer Services Branch, Data User Services Division, U.S. Bureau of the Census, Washington, D.C. 20233	Summary and micro data public use files available	Census of the U.S. Population. Micro data files based on 1/100 or 1/1000 samples.	Public Use Samples available for 1900, 1940, 1950, 1960, 1970, 1980.	General Housing Demographic
Consequences of Childbearing and Childspacing	Margaret Marini, Vanderbilt University	Not in Public Domain	Longitudinal data of 6,338 individuals in high school in 1957-58 and a follow-up of same individuals in 1973-74.	Administered in 1957-58 and same individuals followed-up in 1973-74.	Demographic, Work, Education, Health, Family
Current Population Survey	Customer Services Branch, Data User Services Division, U.S. Bureau of the Census, Washington, D.C. 20233	Public use micro data files.	Multistage probability sample of about 85,000 households.	Conducted monthly since 1940.	Demographic, Employment, Education, Income
Elementary and Secondary Education General Information Survey (ELSEGIS)	Division of Elementary and Secondary Education Statistics, National Center for Education Statistics, Washington, D.C. 20202	Tapes and special tabulations available.	Complete coverage of public and private elementary and secondary education facilities.	Annual surveys since 1968-69.	Education, Expenditures

Table 1. Selected Large-Scale Data Bases (continued)

Title	Contact	Output	Sample Characteristics	Cycles	Key Variables
High School and Beyond	Longitudinal Studies Branch, National Center for Education Statistics, Washington, D.C. 20202	Public use micro data files.	Base year survey included about 58,000 sophomore and senior high school students. Two-year follow-up data on about 30,000 sophomore and 12,000 senior students. Data also obtained from parents and schools.	Base year data collected in 1980 and first follow-up data collected in 1982. This survey builds on the National Longitudinal Study of the High School Class of 1972.	Education, Employment, Income, Occupation Family, Fertility
Higher Education General Information Survey (HEGIS)	University and College Surveys Study Branch, National Center for Education Statistics, Washington, D.C. 20202	Tapes and special tabulation available.	Complete coverage of public and nonpublic 2- and 4-year institutions of higher education.	Annual data since 1966-67.	Education, Expenditures, Occupation
Income Survey Development Program (ISDP)	HHS/ISDP Universal North Building, Room 322B, 1875 Connecticut Avenue, N.W., Washington, D.C. 20009	Public use micro data files available from NTIS.	National sample of about 7,500 households.	All individuals interviewed in 1979 were reinterviewed at 3-month intervals for a total of six interviews.	Consumption, Education, Employment, Family, Household, Income, Marriage, Poverty, Resources Social Services
Individual Income Tax Model File	Individual Income Statistics Section, Internal Revenue Service, Washington, D.C. 20224	Two files are available. One is a national file of all incomes reported. A state version has state codes in all returns and deletes all person records with an income which exceeds $200,000.	Stratified systematic sample of tax returns.	Prepared annually since 1966.	Income
Monitoring the Future Study	Institute for Social Research, University of Michigan, Ann Arbor, MI 48106	Public use micro data files available.	A national sample of up to 300 students selected from about 115 public and 15 private high schools.	Annual series since 1975.	Attributes, Education, Employment, Occupation, Youth
National Assessment of Educational Progress	Educational Testing Service, Princeton, New Jersey	Select micro data files available.	National sample of about 100,000 persons per year. The multistage probability sample of is drawn from the universe 9-, 13-, and 17-year olds, and young adults age 26-35 for a given year.	Starting with 1969-70 school year, every year has seen a study of some of the assessment areas.	Education

Title	Contact	Output	Sample Characteristics	Cycles	Key Variables
National Longitudinal Surveys of Labor Market Experience	Center for Human Resource Research, The Ohio State University, 1375 Perry Street, Columbus, Ohio 43201	Public use micro data files available.	National random samples of six age-sex subsets of the U.S. population. Each sample has about 5,000 individuals.	Two cohorts (1966, 1967) have been repeatedly interviewed since the base year surveys. An additional cohort has been selected since 1979.	Education, Elderly, Employment, Family, Occupation, Resources, Training
Panel Study of Income Dynamics	Inter-University Consortium for Political and Social Science, The University of Michigan, P.O. Box 1248, Ann Arbor, MI 48106	Public use micro data files are available.	Sample of about 5,000 families.	Families and individuals interviewed annually since 1968.	Attitudes, Consumption, Employment, Family, Households Income, Poverty
Project Talent Eleventh Grade Public Use Sample	Machine-Readable Archives Division, National Archives and Records Service, Washington, D.C. 20408	Public use micro data file of the 2,900 individuals in the longitudinal subsample.	Five percent national sample of all students in the 11th grade in 1960. The longitudinal component is a 1/28th subsample of the larger sample.	Base year data collected in 1960 and follow-up interviews for the sub-sample.	Education, Occupation
Survey of Income and Program Participation	Dan Kasprzyk, Population Division, U.S. Bureau of the Census, Washington, D.C. 20233	No data available until late 1984 or 1985.	Nationally representative sample of about 20,000 households.	Initial data collection in 1983 with follow-ups every 4 months for a total of 2 1/2 years for each household.	Demographic, Educational, Family, Income, Program Participation
Seattle and Denver Income Maintenance Experiments	Robert Spiegelman, Research Center, SRI International, 333 Ravenswood Avenue, Menlo Park, CA 94025	Public use micro data file available.	Longitudinal and Cross-sectional data in about 4,800 families (low income families).	Initial data collected in 1970 with repeated interviews between 1970 and 1976.	Demographic, Education, Family, Work
Survey of Income and Education	Paul Siegel or Wendy Bruno, Population Division, U.S. Bureau of the Census, Washington, D.C. 20233	Public use micro data file available.	Nationally representative data on 151,171 households collected in 1976.	Cross-sectional data collected only in 1976.	Demographic, Education, Family, Health
Sustaining Effects Study of Title I	Machine-Readable Archives Division, National Archives and Records Service, Washington, D.C. 20408	Public use micro data files.	Nationally representative sample of about 118,000 elementary school aged students. A subset of students were followed throughout elementary school. In addition, data on parental characteristics for a subsample of the students are available.	Initial data collected in 1976.	Demographic, Educational

works that we have already described, such as Taeuber and Rockwell (1982). There is no data base that meets ideal requirements; therefore, secondary analysis involves compromises.

It makes good sense for policy researchers to draw on resources such as these because it improves the quality of data, reduces costs, and shortens the time required to obtain results. Survey data collection is not only expensive and time-consuming, but it is also a highly technical and labor-intensive endeavor that requires a total research organization, including staff experienced in questionnaire construction and response coding, staff with expertise in sample design and execution, and staff trained in interviewing. In addition, careful attention must be paid to the processing and editing of responses and to the technical aspects of developing large-scale data bases.

This array of skills and personnel calls for a substantial investment of financial and human capital before the first datum is collected. To be sure, one can establish a survey research organization de novo, but the expense and time involved may be far beyond what the usual tightly budgeted research effort can consider. Even if a skilled survey research organization is already available, the cost of interviewing respondents personally has now risen well above $100 per interview, even for efforts that pose only minor problems. This means that data collection for a survey with a small sample of 2,000 persons is likely to cost nearly $250,000. If corners are cut in order to shave costs, the validity and reliability of the data may be threatened.

Clearly, a considerable investment of resources is required. There is no doubt that the federal government has made the required investments on a large scale, since it either created or partially supported some of the finest survey research organizations in the world. These include the Bureau of the Census, the Institute for Social Research (ISR) at the University of Michigan, the National Opinion Research Center (NORC) at the University of Chicago, the Research Triangle Institute (RTI), and the Westat, Inc., to name only a few of the leading organizations. The private sector cannot duplicate the federal government's apparatus for the administrative collection of data, in part because of scale and in part because the government's data-collection activities are built on laws and regulations that mandate compliance and that in many instances exact penalties for providing false information. Policy research can and should draw from the resources that these investments have created, and it often can do so at relatively little cost and in relatively short time. Another advantage of these data bases is that many were collected by disinterested organizations, such as the Bureau of the Census and the major survey research organizations. Federal data are generally accepted as objective and authoritative. Data collected under the direction of an individual policy researcher can more easily be faulted as biased, particularly if the researcher is affiliated with an organization that has an interest in the outcome of the research. Both courts and regulatory agencies are accustomed to working with federally collected data, and they have come to accept secondary analyses of such data as valid research.

As always, there is a price to be paid. Often, the researcher must accommodate his or her ideal research design to the constraints imposed by using data that someone else has collected for different purposes. Also, the confidentiality of survey data often means not only that respondents' names, addresses, and telephone numbers have been stripped from the data bases that are available to the public but also that geographic information has usually been so restricted that the researcher cannot pinpoint places of residence. In many cases, only the state of residence and the relative size of the place of residence (metropolitan, urban, or rural) are provided.

Moreover, details of information are often obscured. For example, reported income levels are often collapsed into only a dozen codes, and the top category is set as low as $50,000 and over in order to protect the privacy of the wealthy. While the effects of these practices can be frustrating to the researcher, they must be borne in good spirit, because the respondent's right to confidentiality is wisely accorded higher priority than the researcher's need for data. This is not to deny that data-collection agencies are sometimes overly zealous, but in any event their conduct is outside the researcher's direct control.

A final word of advice: Before purchasing a data set, the researcher should find out whether the local facility already possesses it. On many university campuses, there is a data librarian who can indicate whether the library has already purchased specific data bases for other researchers. Information may also be obtained from data repositories in the research centers that are housed on many university campuses. Even if these groups do not already own the required data base, they may be able to purchase it at a lower price than the lone researcher if they belong to a consortium, such as the ICPSR. An additional value of finding a research center that has experience with particular large-scale data bases is that the center will have programmers who may be able to assist in the data processing. Programmers who are familiar with specific data bases know the quirks that the documentation sometimes neglects to mention, and they can steer the researcher around problems that they have already encountered.

The researcher who decides to use existing data bases may be

24

tempted to force the research problem to fit these data bases. Usually, some modification or compromise will be needed, or a new analytical approach may be required, but if the data are not what the researcher needs, he or she should not use them just because they are there; research can be undermined by using an inappropriate data source. However, the researcher should take the time to find out, because the rewards may well justify the effort.

References

Borus, M. E. "An Inventory of Longitudinal Data Sets of Interest to Economists." *Review of Public Data Use,* 1982, *10* (1–2), 113–126.
Bowering, D. "Assessing the Impact of Federally Sponsored R&D Expenditures in Science and Engineering on Leading Research Universities and Colleges." In L. Andrew, A. Cuthbert, and L. Nelson (Eds.), *Research in Postsecondary Education: Utilization of HEGIS and Other National Data Bases.* Blacksburg: College of Education, Virginia Polytechnic Institution and State University, 1982.
David, M. "Access to Data: The Frustration and Utopia of the Researcher." *Review of Public Data Use,* 1980, *8* (4), 327–337.
Dodd, S. A. *Cataloging Machine-Readable Data Files: An Interpretive Manual.* Chicago: American Library Association, 1982.
Hyman, H. H. *Secondary Analysis of Sample Surveys: Principles, Procedures, and Potentialities.* New York: Wiley, 1972.
Inter-university Consortium for Political and Social Research (ICPSR). *Guide to Resources and Services.* Ann Arbor, Mich.: ICPSR, 1983.
Inter-university Consortium for Political and Social Research (ICPSR). *CJAIN Bulletin.* (Periodic newsletter.) Ann Arbor, Mich.: ICPSR.
Inter-university Consortium for Political and Social Research (ICPSR). *NACDA Bulletin.* (Periodic newsletter.) Ann Arbor, Mich.: ICPSR.
Louis Harris Political Data Center, University of North Carolina. *Directory of Louis Harris Public Opinion Machine-Readable Data.* Chapel Hill, N.C.: Institute for Research in Social Science, 1981.
Louis Harris Political Data Center, University of North Carolina. *Sourcebook of Harris National Surveys: Repeated Questions 1963–1976.* Chapel Hill, N.C,: Institute for Research in Social Science, 1981.
Prewitt, K. "Counting and Accountability: Numbers, the Social Sciences, and Democracy." In Social Science Research Council, *Annual Report 1982–1983.* New York: Social Science Research Council, 1983.
Public Archives, Canada. "Citation of Machine Readable Data Files." *Bulletin of the Machine Readable Archives,* 1983, *1* (3), 1–2.
Roper Center for Public Opinion Research, The University of Connecticut. *A Guide to Roper Center Resources for the Study of American Race Relations.* Storrs, Conn.: The Roper Center, Inc., 1982.
Roper Center for Public Opinion Research, Williams College; and the Social Science Research Council. *Survey Data for Trend Analysis: An Index to Repeated Questions in U.S. National Surveys Held by the Roper Public Opinion Research Center.* Williamstown, Mass.: The Roper Center, 1975. (Available only from ERIC Document Reproduction Service.)
Roper Center for Public Opinion Research, The University of Connecticut. *Data Set News.* (Periodic newsletter.) Storrs, Conn.: The Roper Center.

Taeuber, R. C., and Rockwell, R. C. "National Social Data Series: A Compendium of Brief Descriptions." *Review of Public Data Use,* 1982, *10* (1-2), 23-111.

Turner, C. F., and Martin, E. (Eds.). *Surveys of Subjective Phenomena: Summary Report.* Washington, D.C.: National Academy Press, 1981.

U.S. Bureau of the Census. *Bureau of the Census Catalog 1982-1983.* Washington, D.C.: U.S. Government Printing Office, 1983.

U.S. National Archives and Records Service. *Catalog of Machine-Readable Records in the National Archives of the United States.* Washington, D.C.: National Archives and Records Service, 1983.

U.S. National Technical Information Service (NTIS). *A Directory of Federal Statistical Data Files.* Prepared by the U.S. Department of Commerce, Office of Federal Statistical Policy and Standards (out of existence). Springfield, Va: NTIS, 1981.

David E. Myers is senior analyst at Decision Resources Corporation, Washington, D.C., and works in the policy evaluation and analytic studies group.

Richard C. Rockwell is staff associate with the Social Science Research Council in New York, where he works with the Council's program in quantitative research and statistics. He is also chairman of the Committee on National Statistics of the American Sociological Association.

After a data base has been located and tapes obtained, the necessary files must be set up to analyze the data. The newcomer to secondary analysis is led carefully through the technical requirements of file preparation, from data verification to variable definition.

Considerations and Methodology for the Preparation of Data Files

Jim C. Fortune
Janice K. McBee

The case for secondary analysis of extant data bases can be based both on the cost-effectiveness of such research and on the contribution that it can make to the behavioral sciences (Bryant and Wortman, 1978). Data collection represents the major cost in most behavioral science research. Frequently, the cost and the complexity of large-scale data collection are major deterrents to the conduct of generalizable research in education and psychology. Too often, studies are limited to parochial subpopulations or convenient samples in order to avoid large-scale data collection. Data archives can supply some of the needed data.

The contributions of secondary analysis is evident in the growing list of uses to which this emerging methodology has been put. Boruch (1978) provides an excellent introduction to secondary analysis, which has been used to investigate methodological problems in the analysis of field-based research data, to conduct metaevaluations and alternative analyses of evaluative data, to study policy implications

D. J. Bowering (Ed.). *Secondary Analysis of Available Data Bases.* New Directions for Program Evaluation, no. 22. San Francisco: Jossey-Bass, June 1984.

and alternatives, to extend data archives to new problem areas, and to synthesize evaluation and research on a given topic or problem. However, all these uses represent only the tip of the iceberg. Secondary analysis has many more potential uses.

This emerging methodology has encountered certain difficulties — gaining access to data bases, acquiring adequate documentation of these data bases, and protecting privacy and proprietary rights. These difficulties have been documented, and they are being addressed by the profession (Bryant and Wortman, 1978). This chapter addresses another problem area, the complexity of data file preparation.

Secondary analysis can be described as a sequence of nine research steps: identifying a problem of interest, finding appropriate data bases, negotiating access to these data bases, obtaining data tapes, designing the study of interest, preparing the required data file, accessing the variables of interest, analyzing the data, and reporting the results. Each step can be delineated further into a series of tasks that the researcher must complete. The tasks that delineate steps one, five, seven, and nine are spelled out in most research methodology texts. The tasks that delineate steps two, three, and four are logistical tasks that these texts seldom describe. The tasks that delineate step six combine computer mechanics and research methodology. The difficulty and complexity of this step and the nature of the tasks that are required to complete it depend on the condition of the primary data bases.

On the surface, the creation of a data file appears to be a simple mechanical process involving the reading of data from magnetic tapes; sometimes, it also involves the transfer of these data to disc or tape. Under ideal circumstances, this process may be all that is required to create the data file. However, deviations from the ideal can complicate the process. Depending on the circumstances, several different processes may be required to prepare data files. For instance, file preparation may require the merging of two or more primary data bases, the addition of new data collected either for file expansion purposes or for sample extension purposes to a primary data base, the modification of a primary data base by changing its organizational structure or by changing the specificity of its data, or the modification of a primary data base by imputation or file deletion.

For each of these processes, design considerations increase the complexity of the overall process. Some are based on the conditions of the primary data bases, while others are based on research requirements of the file to be created. Design considerations associated with the conditions of the primary data bases involve four issues: whether the data bases to be merged are censuses of the same population or of similar populations, whether the data bases to be merged are in the form of a census of a population or a sample of the same or similar population, whether the data bases to be merged are samples of the same or of similar populations, or whether a single primary data base requires modifications or not. Design considerations associated with research requirements of the file to be created involve four other issues: whether the study is to include projections of the data to a universe, whether the study is to generate simple descriptions of the status of the data, whether the study is to include cross sectional comparisons of the data, and whether the study is to include longitudinal comparisons of the data.

The conditions of the primary data bases and the research requirements of the file to be created interact to create a unique array of pitfalls involving data loss, documentation problems, and data anomalies. Frequently, the construction of a data file requires the researcher to make decisions about data that go beyond current research methodology. For instance, sampling methodology does not provide solutions for some problems encountered in file merger, measurement theory fails to provide methodology for handling some transformations and modifications of variables, and statistics offers no analytical models for the analysis of some resulting data configurations. In these cases, the researcher must make a decision without the guidance of research methodology. Although the effects of these decisions on the final research results can often not be estimated, their rationale should be documented for the information of the research consumer. All in all, both the quality of the data file and the validity of the secondary analysis depend on the care, the accuracy, and the thoroughness with which the data file is prepared and on the quality of the primary data bases.

Data File Requirements and Data Base Characteristics

What takes place in the preparation of a data file depends on the nature of the primary data base and on the design of the secondary analysis. The activities that take place in file preparation are made up of different sequences of six preparation tasks: file verification, sample verification, file merger, data aggregation, file modification, and variable construction. Analysis of the interaction of varying conditions of the primary data base and various study requirements reveals more than a dozen types of file preparations or sequences of these six tasks. In addition to the sequences of tasks associated with the different types of file preparation, there are also some pitfalls. The first step in describing data file preparation is to identify the information that the researcher must possess about data file requirements and about the primary data base. The second step is to describe the pitfalls that confound the preparation process.

How User Tapes Are Archived. Much of the secondary analysis numbers on the list fit the definitions. To verify the coding or scaling number of events are associated with this activity: large-scale federal programming in education, notable shifts and depression in the economy, the civil rights movement, the emergence of the contract research world, large-scale federal surveys and evaluations, and the rapid growth of the computer industry. Prior to this increased activity in secondary analysis, only a few farsighted researchers expressed much interest in secondary analysis, and there were few sources from which data bases could be obtained. Then and now, the two major sources for extant data bases are the National Archives of the United States and the U.S. Bureau of the Census. However, as a result of the increased interest in secondary analysis, several other agencies, such as the National Center for Education Statistics, the National Institute of Education, and the National Science Foundation, are now creating user tapes of archived data.

Usually, user tapes range in cost between $100 and $200. The tapes are available in serveral formats: seven- or nine-track 1,600 or 6,250 bytes per inch; EBCDIC or ASCII code; labeled or unlabeled; and odd or even parity. The potential user must compare the requirements of his or her computer with the system specifications in which the user tapes are available. If the two systems are not compatible, the potential user must locate a computer facility that is compatible to both. In some cases, the user tapes have been formatted so that they can be used with such statistical software packages as SPSS (Nie and others, 1975), BMD (Dixon and Brown, 1979), or SAS (Helwig and Council, 1979). In most cases, the tapes include basic formatting information, and they are accompanied by technical documentation, which is sometimes available on microfiche and at other times in print. Generally, the technical documentation includes a summary of the tape's content (number of records, record length, and selected frequencies), a description of the file organization, a description of the sampling (if necessary), a list of the variables, a description of how each variable is coded, a format of the data, a bibliography of references, and information about user services. Frequently, the technical documentation neglects to provide information on data abnormalities or on missing data, and field notes concerning data collection are often missing. Often copies of the data collection instruments have to be requested from the agency responsible for the user tapes. In cases where data are deemed confidential, identification codes are assigned to respondents in order to protect their privacy, and the assignment algorithms are not released by the agencies.

Influence of File Requirements. Some characteristics of study design require special considerations in the preparation of data files. These considerations tend to differ if the data to be used in the preparation of data tapes come from a single data base or from two or more data bases. Certainly, any design requirement influences the construction of new data files. The influence of these requirements will not be discussed here. Here, we will examine only those design requirements that call for additional actions on the part of the researcher in preparing the data file. Six design requirements appear to influence data file preparation in unique ways: describing the status of a sample on selected characteristics, projecting from a sample to a universe, making cross sectional comparisons, making longitudinal comparisons, changing the unit of analysis or the unit on which file cases are organized, and constructing variables.

Describing the Status of a Sample on Selected Populations. A design that seeks to describe the status of a sample on selected characteristics creates two types of special considerations in secondary analysis: verification of the time of data collection and verification of the population represented by the sample. Although the time of data collection is important in any secondary analysis, it becomes especially sensitive when the purpose of secondary analysis is to describe the status of a sample on selected characteristics. To illustrate, if the sample characteristic being described is school achievement, then the month in which achievement is measured becomes meaningful. If the sample whose status is being described comes from a single data base, then the referent population should be easy to identify, provided that the documentation is adequate. However, if the sample is an intersection of two or more data bases, then the researcher must attempt to define the hypothetical population that the sample represents. To put it another way, the reseacher must identify in what way data loss has biased the sample; that is, the researcher must identify underrepresented aspects of the sample and overrepresented aspects of the sample.

Projecting a Sample to a Universe. Secondary analysis can also seek to describe the status of a universe on selected characteristics from a sample. The task is similar to that just described for the description of the status of a sample on selection characteristics, and it entails all the special considerations in file preparation just discussed. However, the projection process in the design involves one additional requirement that must be met when the data file is prepared: Weights that allow an unbiased estimation of the population for which the sample was shown to be representative must be developed for each sample unit. Generation of such weights allows population totals and marginals to be estimated across a subset of the variables in the primary data bases.

Making Cross Sectional Comparisons. The making of cross sectional comparisons in secondary analysis also requires additional considerations in preparation of the data file. These considerations apply primarily when the data come from two or more data bases. They are directed toward establishment of the comparability of the two cohort groups on data characteristics that may affect the dependent variable. These data characteristics include the appropriateness of the times of data collection, the equality of the two sampling fractions, the congruence of the referent populations, the uniformity of measurement of the dependent variable in the two data bases, and the definition of the unit of analysis in the two data bases — it must be identical. Many of these verification tasks require information that the usual technical documentation does not supply. Thus, consultation with someone who knows the data base is mandatory. The investigation of sample characteristics will necessitate reference to population statistics.

Making Longitudinal Comparisons. Longitudinal comparisons in secondary analysis increase the complexity of file preparation when the file is to be constructed from two or more primary data bases. The effects of data loss in the merger of the two data bases make establishment of the representativeness of the sample a major consideration. Two different types of preparation are possible when a longitudinal file is constructed from two or more primary data bases. One type occurs when pretest information is in one primary data base and posttest information is in another. This configuration often occurs in the analysis of annual reports. The other occurs when both data bases have pretest and posttest information on the same dependent variable on different samples of the same or similar populations. This configuration often occurs in large-scale evaluations. In the first type of preparation, the researcher must match respondents across files. This task requires one of three sequences of actions: direct matching of respondents' identification code numbers; conversion of code numbers in one primary data base into code numbers in the second data base, followed by matching of respondents; or matching respondents by comparing several matching characteristics present in both data bases (the nesting of these characteristics provides an unique number for each case). If one or both data bases are developed on a census of a population, then the data loss in merger and matching is restricted to nonrespondents. However, if the two primary data bases are constructed on independent samples, then the data loss can be expected to be considerable, and the researcher must establish that sufficient data can be merged to conduct the analysis or that the remaining sample can be construed to be representative of a nontrivial population. If the planned analyses involve multiple classifications of the data, then this consideration becomes critical. In the first type of file preparation, the researcher must also establish that the difference between the time of year in which the pretest and the posttest occurred and the time elapsed between the two permit meaningful comparisons to be made. In the second type of file preparation, the researcher must establish that the two data bases use identical definitions for the unit of analysis and, if they are different, for the respondents as well; that the same respondents are not included in both primary data bases, in which case they would appear twice in the new file; that the time of pretesting is relatively equal across the data bases; and that the time elapsed between pretest and posttest is similar across the merged sample components. For both types of file preparation, the researcher must establish that there is uniformity of measurement of the dependent, independent, and mediating variables across the merged sample components.

Changing Units of Analysis and Units of Organization. In secondary analysis, design requirements that call for changes in the unit of analysis or in the unit on which the primary data file is organized mandate special considerations in file preparation. These considerations differ for data aggregation and data disaggregation. If the change in units involves data aggregation, the researcher must establish that the subunits are adequately and evenly represented for each aggregate unit and that there are no effects from ecological inference or differential grouping rules across the aggregate units. If the change of units involves data disaggregation, the researcher must ascertain that inclusion of the new units does not bias the sample. If data external to the primary data bases are used in the disaggregation process, then the researcher must establish both that these external data are appropriate and that they create no bias.

Constructing Variables. The last design requirement that influences the preparation of data files involves the construction of variables. Several techniques are used to construct variables. The choice of a technique depends on the definition and specification of the new variable and on the distributions and nature of the primary data. In most cases, for each technique used with continuous data there exists an analogue for categorical data. Data file preparation considerations differ across techniques. Generally, the reseacher must investigate the distributions of the primary data and make appropriate adjustments when selecting techniques for construction of variables. Then, the researcher must prepare the primary data so that the technique selected can be applied. Depending on the particular technique that is selected, preparation of the primary data can involve data transformations, creation of standard scores, or the combination of items or parts of items; in some cases, preliminary steps are not required. The distributions of the new variable should be checked, and only then should the new variable be added to the data file.

Knowledge Required About User Tapes. The preparation of data files requires knowledge about the layout of user tapes and about the data processing of the primary data. The knowledge required about the layout of the user tape includes the number of tracks on the tape (seven or nine), the magnetic recording codes (BCD, EBCDIC, or ASCII), the number of bytes per inch (650, 800, 1,600, or 6,250), data storage (packed or not), parity (odd or even), the number of files, the number of characters or elements per file, blocking, labeling, and whether the user tape has been preformatted for use with one of the statistical packages. The knowledge required about the data processing includes whether the data file includes commented instructions, whether the data file includes value and variable labels, the unit on which cases are organized, the identification code for each case, whether the different types of respondents are nested in each case or not and how many respondents of each type there are, how identification codes are assigned to respondents, what variables are included in each case, how variables are formatted, how each variable is coded, how nonresponse has been handled, how missing data have been handled, and whether cases contain alphanumerics or blanks. Hofeditz (1979) provides a short, helpful guide to these issues. Any computer center has materials on tape-handling procedures.

Influence of Primary Data Base Characteristics. Several characteristics of the primary data base influence the preparation of data files: the contents of the technical documentation, the number of data bases, the nature of the design in which the data were developed, nonresponse and missing data, information on data edits, the specificity of data coding, the distribution of variables, identification of respondents, and the complexity of the variables measured.

The contents of the technical documentation determine whether contact with individuals who have firsthand knowledge of the data is required in order to prepare data files, the extent to which the researcher must conduct a descriptive study of the primary data, and whether the researcher must investigate the measurement and data collection efforts by which the data were gathered.

The number of the data bases in which the primary data are located determines the extent to which the researcher must be concerned about differences in definition and measurement of variables across the data bases, the differences in case organization and respondent identification, the differences across the data bases in sampling design and response rates, the number of different tape specifications and file configurations with which the researcher must contend, and the differences in time and method of data collection across the data bases.

The nature of the design in which the data were developed provides information about their characteristics and shortcomings. If the data were developed through a survey, then they are likely to come from a sample, they are likely to be categorical (both nominal and ordinal), they may require weighting in order to be representative of a population, they are not likely to have both pretest and posttest data, and they may be subject to bias created by nonresponse and missing data. If the data were developed in an evaluation, then they are likely to be both continuous and categorical, to come from several respondents, to include both pretest and posttest data, and to be subject to bias created by guarded responses. If the data were developed through a reporting system, then the data are likely to come from a census, which reduces the problems created by nonresponse; they are likely to suffer from bias created by guarded responses; and they possess the characteristics of survey data. If the data were developed through a quasi-experimental design, then they are likely to possess design controls, they are less susceptible to bias from guarded response than evaluation data are, and they are similar in composition to evaluative data.

Nonresponse and missing data require the researcher to identify the source of the resulting biases and the resultant referent population. The researcher must also determine whether there are sufficient data for certain analyses, and the researcher must calculate weights if they are deemed necessary.

Information on edits of the primary data allows the researcher to avoid a total edit. It also allows the researcher to determine whether further edits are required and to trust that there are no mechanical errors on the user tape.

The specificity of data coding allows the researcher to determine what tasks must be completed to match variable definitions, to link file cases, to construct variables, and to modify file organization.

Information about the distribution of variables in the primary data permits the researcher to identify inaccurate data on specific variables, to determine whether files can be merged and respondents can be linked, to determine whether certain techniques can be used in the construction of variables, and to determine whether certain data classifications can be made and certain analyses can be performed.

Identification of respondents is essential for the creation of longitudinal data files, for some tape mergers, for some file modifications, and for the use of certain techniques for the construction of variables.

The complexity of the variables measured determines the difficulty in modifying file organization, the difficulty in constructing variables, the difficulty in identifying and handling different types of respondents, the difficulty in identifying the referent population, the difficulty in aggregating or disaggregating data, the likelihood of data collection misuses, and the likelihood of data processing errors.

Pitfalls in Data File Preparation. The pitfalls in data file preparation can be grouped under seven heads: sample skews, merger mortality, nonresponse noise, variant variables, aggregate anomalies, time tangles, and mechanical misuses. These pitfalls originate in the data processing and in the construction of the data file required to conduct the planned study. Since they threaten the validity of the secondary analysis, the possibility of encountering these pitfalls should be considered when deciding whether the study can or should be conducted.

Sample Skews. Sample skews occur when data bases are merged, when data with missing values are used to construct variables, when nonresponse and item nonresponse are not reported, when data weights are incorrect, and when oversampling is not reported. Sample skews can be defined as the over- or underrepresentation of some segment of a population under study. When data bases are merged to create a longitudinal file or when the number of variables in the file for each case is extended, there are cases on one data base for which matching cases cannot be found on the second data base. These unmatched cases drop out of the study, which can cause a sample skew in the data base to be used for the secondary analysis. When one of the variables or data elements for which values are missing is included in a variable-construction effort, the missing data can cause fallacious values to be computed for the new variable. The erroneous estimation can serve to create a sample skew on the new variable. When nonresponse is disproportionate for a given segment of a population on one or more variables, the result is a sample skew. Similarly, if the weights assigned some respondents in a weighted sample are too large, then there is sample skew in the projection to the population. Since weighting is based on population totals, overweighting of some respondents results in underweighting of others. In large-scale data bases, minority groups or other subgroups of the population are often oversampled to allow special studies to be conducted. If the primary data bases do not contain a method that allows the oversampled subgroups to be identified, then a sample skew is created for any study of the data base.

Merger Mortality. Merger mortality occurs when a large or disproportionate segment of a population has to be dropped from the data file on which the study is to be conducted. Segments of the population are dropped from the data file when nonmatching occurs in file mergers, when a change in the unit of file organization creates disproportionality, and when a researcher attempts to reduce sample skew. Three threats result from merger mortality: First, redefinition of the referent population through data loss can render the study population trivial or uninteresting. Second, inadequate sample sizes can eliminate significant differences from the analysis. Third, a reduction of the number of classifications in the analysis due to small sample sizes can create specification errors.

Nonresponse Noise. Nonresponse noise occurs when nonresponse is systematic or disproportionate, when the reason for nonresponse cannot be determined, and when its effect cannot be estimated. When nonresponse noise is large, it can cause a potential finding to go undetected either by failing to measure subjects who hold a specific value of a variable or by increasing the error term in a given analysis. Even when nonresponse noise is small, it can create subtle influences by reducing the size of group differences or by changing the direction of small group differences.

Variant Variables. Variant variables occur when there are slight differences in the definitions of a variable across two data bases or when the variable is coded in different ways in two data bases. Slight differences in definitions across data bases can cause the variable under consideration to be measured on different metrics. This biases the results. Differences in coding across data bases can cause an estimation error for the variable.

Aggregate Anomalies. Aggregate anomalies occur when the unit of analysis and the level at which measurement occurred are different or when the organizational unit used to create a new data file is different from the one in the primary data base. In both cases, the error stems from the nesting and aggregation of data. To illustrate, students are nested in classrooms, classrooms are nested in schools, and schools are nested in districts. If schools are the unit of analysis and if the dependent variable is reading achievement, then students' reading achievement scores must be aggregated to school level by averaging. Error in data aggregation can occur in two ways. The first way is through ecological inference or the effects of differential grouping. In this case, the use of averages as data points of upper-level units results in the loss of variance, which occurs more in some units than it does in others. The second way in which error occurs in aggregation is through non-response or sampling abnormalities, which cause nested units across the upper-level units to be unevenly represented.

Time Tangles. Time tangles occur when two data bases with time discrepancies are merged. Error can occur in two ways. The first way involves a discrepancy in the time of data collection across data bases that affects key variables of interest in the study. To illustrate, let us imagine that the secondary analysis wishes to compare achievement data across two data bases. If the data in the first data base were collected toward the end of an academic year and the data in the second data base were collected at the beginning of the academic year, the resulting analysis will be flawed. The second way occurs when data bases in which the time elapsed between pretest and posttest is different are merged. If six months elapse between pre- and posttesting in one data base and nine months elapse in the other, the two data bases cannot be compared.

Mechanical Misuses. Mechanical misuses can be defined as human errors that affect data processing and computer mechanics. There are several places in the file-preparation process where human error can occur. Pitfalls of this nature include premature truncation of a data file or variable, misreading of a format or a code, mislocation of transferred data, combinations of the wrong variables, invalid algorithms, transcription errors, and inadequate edits.

Considerations in Data File Preparation

Researchers who are not experienced in secondary analysis often view data file preparation as a simple mechanical process. The discussion in the preceding section shows that the process can vary in its complexity and that it contains several pitfalls. There are some considerations that the researcher can take that will help to assure success in data file preparation.

Overview of the Preparation Process. Data file preparation varies both in its complexity and in the number of activities that must be performed in order to construct the required data file. The research requirements of the secondary analysis and the characteristics of the primary data bases determine the activities required for this task. The data file preparation process can be described in twenty-nine generic steps. These steps can be reduced to eight in the simplest case. In the most complex cases, many more than twenty-nine may be required, depending on the number of file modifications and variable constructions that are involved. These are the twenty-nine basic steps:

1. Review the secondary analysis plan to generate a list of research design requirements for the new data file.
2. Review the characteristics of the primary data bases in the light of these file requirements, and develop a list of file preparation considerations.
3. Identify and list the pitfalls that may be involved in preparation of the new file.
4. Develop a list of specifications for the data file, including sample requirements, required variables, measurement requirements, analysis requirements, and so forth.
5. Review the documentation available for the primary data bases, noting any data base characteristics that may prevent data file specifications from being met.
6. Obtain and review other relevant background information about the primary data bases, including time of collection, prior uses, errata, and so forth.
7. Run frequencies of selected variables on the user tape, and match output with documentation summaries to verify that the tape is as it has been described.
8. Review design factors in primary data bases to identify sampling design, nonresponse, missing data, variables included, formatting and coding of variables, and so forth.
9. Compare primary data base design factors with file specifications to identify needed file modifications and variables to be constructed.
10. Outline and sequence the list of tasks required to prepare the data file.
11. Conduct any additional edits that are required and the preliminary distribution analysis of the primary data bases, noting nonresponse distribution, missing data, abnormal distributions, unmatched coding, and so forth.
12. Obtain outside information for marginal data checks if possible. Otherwise, seek the judgments of experts in the area of study in order to obtain estimates of data marginals.
13. Use the results of the analysis of variable definitions and primary data distributions to revise the list of tasks required to prepare the data file.

14. Conduct data base mergers if necessary to obtain the variables required.
15. Run frequencies of selected variables relevant to the planned secondary analysis.
16. Analyze data loss, and identify the referent population.
17. Obtain external information relevant to the referent population, and conduct data checks.
18. Revise tasks required for file preparation and the study design, given the nature of the available data.
19. Conduct file modifications if necessary.
20. Run frequencies on selected variables after file modification, and check them with frequencies run on the merged data base.
21. Analyze data loss and new distributions of variables, and check for aggregation effects.
22. Seek external information or expertise to check on the reasonableness of the resulting data aggregates and new units.
23. Revise tasks required for file preparation and the study design, given the nature of the file modifications.
24. Construct new variables if necessary.
25. Run frequencies for new variables, and check them with variables calculated by hand for a small number of cases.
26. Develop the new file, and document its characteristics after checking the accuracy of the data transfer and file-producing mechanics.
27. Compare file characteristics with the study's design requirements.
28. Revise the study and the study requirements so as to match the final form of the data file.
29. Document the data file preparation process, and ready the new file for secondary analysis.

Role of Compromise. The final design represents a compromise between the extent to which a file can be constructed from existing data bases and the specifications of the file required by the design of the secondary analysis. As a result, the secondary analysis that is conducted is often not the secondary analysis that was planned. The difference between the actual study and the planned study depends on the degree to which the data bases prevent construction of the data file that the researcher desires. Even if the original objectives have to be compromised, it seems preferable to accomplish less with appropriate data than it is to reduce the study's credibility with caveats.

The Importance of Getting to Know the Data

If the researcher who prepares the data file has only a superficial knowledge of the primary data bases, then the pitfalls involved in file preparation possess their greatest likelihood of affecting the study's results. Hence, the researcher needs to know the primary data bases. The researcher needs information about five things: prior uses of the primary data, errata, how and when the primary data were collected, organizational units and data format, and sources of information that can be used as external data checks.

Prior Uses. Knowledge of the prior uses of primary data can provide pertinent information about potential response bias associated with the purpose of the agency for which the data were collected, relationships between variables in the data base, and history that may have affected the data collection. Frequently, the agency responsible for the data has a complete or near complete bibliography of the prior uses of the data bases. In the case where two or more data bases are used as primary data, the comparison of the consistency of the performance of variables across the data bases is useful in determining which pitfalls are most likely to be encountered.

Errata. Usually, the agencies that provide user tapes maintain lists of errors in the data bases if researchers report them. Frequently, the researcher can obtain errata for the data bases that he or she plans to use in file preparation. In other cases, errors can be discovered through conversations with someone in the agency who knows the primary data base. Knowledge of errors permits the researcher to make corrections at the beginning of the process and to identify errors that might otherwise require an effort to find.

How and When Data Were Collected. Knowledge concerning the data collection instruments, mode, history, and time is essential for preparation of data files. Frequently, a combination of sources must be used to reconstruct the data-collection process. The documentation usually includes an overview of the data-collection process. However, this description needs to be supplemented by the data-collection instruments, which can be obtained from the agency, and by the information on the time of data collection, which can be obtained in part from the documentation and in part from discussions with agency personnel who know the data base. The time information is especially critical in file mergers.

Units, Coding, and Format. Data handling often creates fallacies for secondary analysis that can go undetected until the planned study is completed. Slight differences in the definition of units, variables, and populations can cause the researcher to think that two different elements are the same. The same or a similar variable across two data bases by different codes (1 = males and 2 = females in one data base and the opposite in another) or by using a different metric can result in a similar combination error. Mechanical error can occur if the data are formatted incorrectly. Hence, detailed analysis of the definitions, coding, and format of the primary data base is essential in file preparation. The documentation provides information on the definitions, codes, and format. However, verifying this information by conducting runs on the user tape prior to merger is strongly recommended.

External Information Sources. To identify erroneous files and to control the quality of the file preparation process, the contents of the primary data base can be compared with information from external sources. Steps 7, 12, 17, and 22 of the file preparation process require information from external sources. Often, such information is available through the Bureau of the Census, related agencies, and library services. Sowell and Casey (1982) compare these library services in a useful appendix.

Aids in File Preparation

Since the difficulty of the file-preparation process is sometimes underestimated and since some parts of the process require researcher logic rather than tradition-tested methodology, the researcher who develops the file needs all the help that he or she can get. There are four aids on which the researcher can rely: the documentation for the primary data base, backup provisions in case of machine or researcher error, packaged statistical programs, and agency user services.

Primary Data Base Documentation. The documentation for primary data bases is usually developed in accordance with agency requirements but it is always written specifically for the data base that it documents. Sometimes, agency conventions make file documentation difficult to interpret. Hence, the first-time user of a given user tape may have to contact the agency in order to learn about the agency's documentation conventions. Data base documentation is a frequent reference in the file preparation process.

Backup Provisions. In the days when most computer work required punched cards, experienced researchers developed backup provisions, such as duplicate data decks, card-numbering codes that controlled card sequence, color coding that allowed card files to be kept together, and box labels that controlled data entry. These backup provisions were developed to prevent disaster if a card reader mutilated some cards, if a card deck was dropped, or if the contents of card boxes were entered into the machine in the wrong order. Similar backup provisions can be made for machine handling of tapes by keeping a backup or duplicate tape at the product stage of the process. Backup tapes and documentation free researchers from system or process errors that would otherwise require them to begin the process all over again.

Packaged Statistical Programs. The reading, duplicating, and transcribing of tapes require relatively simple computer programming, which can be written in a short time. However, statistical routines and data transformation routines generally require more complex programming, and considerable time and effort may be required to develop and test such programs. Thus, the flexible, proven, packaged statistical programs that have become available in recent years are helpful to researchers. Three are in common use: BMD (Dixon and Brown, 1979), SPSS (Nie and others, 1975), and SAS (Helwig and Council, 1979). Most university computer systems, government agency computer systems, commercial computer services, and large private systems make one or more of these packaged statistical programs available to users. Manuals for these systems can be purchased at technical book stores or from the publishers. These packages make reliable computer routines easily and quickly available to researchers.

Agency User Services. Many agencies that provide user tapes have established user services to facilitate use of the archived data that they can supply. These user services usually handle the purchasing and distribution of user tapes. They also provide information about tapes on request, and they link users with file experts. It is often necessary to contact agency user services when preparing data files.

Methodology of File Preparation

The methodology of file preparation includes six families of techniques: file verification, sample verification, file merger, data aggregation, file modification, and variable construction. Each family of techniques is composed of several methods, whose appropriateness depends on the requirements of the task and on the characteristics of the data. The primary methods in each family of techniques will be reviewed here. For more detailed descriptions, the reader should consult the references cited.

File-Verification Techniques. File-verification techniques involve procedures that allow the researcher to be confident that the primary data base is as it has been described. To some extent, file-verification techniques consist of the systematic application of common sense, which is already used in some research activities, such as field methodology (Douglas, 1976). From another perspective, file-verification techniques involve the application of exploratory (Tukey, 1977) and descriptive (Bartz, 1971) statistics. Several verification tasks are involved in file preparation: checking file contents, checking formats, checking the file's completeness, comparing definitions of variables, comparing the coding of variables, and analyzing distributions.

The checking of file contents requires the researcher to determine whether the variables specified in the documentation are present in the file, whether the summary statistics given in the documentation for these variables can be replicated from the user tape or tapes in hand, and whether the file contains the number of cases or records reported in the documentation. A complementary task is to find out how nonresponses and missing data are handled in the data base. Users of archival files often find that the variables are out of order in the file. Hence, a check of descriptive statistics on each variable will prevent mistakes in order and format. Sometimes, there are discrepancies between the number of cases or records actually on the file and the number reported in the documentation. Any discrepancy, no matter how small, is cause for major concern. Most often, the discrepancy indicates either that all the data are not on the tape or that the tape does not contain the data described in the documentation. Frequently, user tapes have the same format for different data bases. In both cases, the researcher should find out what is wrong before continuing with the file preparation process. Format errors are another source of discrepancies between file documentation and tape readings. It is easy to truncate a variable by omitting a column in the format or by miscounting the number of variables or the number of columns in a format. Again, the verification process involves running the data and checking the documentation information.

A second group of verification activities involves the definition and the coding or scaling of variables. To verify the definitions of variables, the researcher must first review the descriptions in the documentation. Then, the researcher must list the values for the variables of interest in the total file or in a sample of the file and see whether the numbers on the list fit the definitions. To verify the coding or scaling of a variable, the researcher uses frequencies run from the tape to check compliance with the code or scale ranges. Distribution analyses can be used to verify that the data satisfy the statistical assumptions of the analyses that are planned or that they meet the requirements established for the construction of variables. Definitions and coding of variables must be compared across primary data files before the files can be merged.

Sample-Verification Techniques. Sample-verification techniques are needed during the exploratory stage of file preparation, after each data base merger, after file modification, and after construction of variables. Sample-verification processes include investigating the degree to which the primary data bases reflect the sampling procedures described in the documentation; investigating the extent to which nonresponse, data loss, and missing data affect the data base; and estimating the effect that nonresponse, data loss, and missing data have on the data base.

To investigate the degree to which the primary data bases reflect sampling procedures described in the documentation, the researcher must determine whether the data base could have been generated by the sampling plan described in the documentation. One method of making this determination is to use population statistics to calculate a simulated sample and see whether the characteristics of this sample resemble those of the data base. Another method is to begin with the data base and estimate sample parameters, such as the sampling fraction and proportions, and then to compare these estimates with the values appearing in the documentation.

To investigate the extent of nonresponse, data loss, and missing data, the researcher compares the data base with the expected frequencies calculated from population statistics. This process can be complex, since the identity of the original nonrespondents may not be available to the researcher. Three alternative methods exist for this investigation. The first method uses a series of cross tabulations to identify proportions of certain subsamples in the data base. These proportions can then be compared with population proportions across the same variables. The second method involves the development of a matrix defined by several key variables or descriptors of the population and the calculation of frequency of response and the expected responses for each cell of the matrix. When the data base is compared with the original sample of the population, the sampling fraction or proportions used to estimate the expected responses are those that the documentation reports. When the comparison is made after file merger, file modification, or construction of variables, the sample parameters can be estimated with a ratio formed by the total remaining response and the population statistics. Comparison of the overall matrix can be made within cells and across marginals. The third method estimates sample parameters and uses cross validation principles to apply these estimated sample parameters to the population statistics in order to generate several simulated samples. The researcher must then determine whether the remaining data base approximates any of the simulated samples. If one of the three methods shows substantial discrepancies, then the researcher may wish to redefine the referent population, or he or she may wish to remove some elements from the overpopulated cells.

To estimate the effects of nonresponse, missing data, and data loss on selected variables, the researcher can choose from several methods. These methods range from regression techniques and imputation techniques to sampling theory and probability techniques. Descriptions of these methods can be found in Kish (1965), Cohen and Cohen (1975), and Cook and Campbell (1979). Kish (1965) presents an excellent treatment of nonresponse error.

File Merger Techniques. File merger involves the development of computer algorithms to compare successive elements of two data bases by their record identification numbers. If the file organization units in either data base lack identification numbers, then matching principles will have to be applied to both data bases in order to create comparative identification codes for the records that they contain. The application of matching techniques involves the selection of several variables in each record that are common to both data bases. Values of these variables should identify records uniquely when combined either through summation or through simple stringing of columns. These calculated codes can then be used as identification codes for the merger. In some cases, the records in the two data bases use different identification codes. In such cases, the two codes have to be converted into one. This can be accomplished by developing an input file that records one code into the other or by developing a formula that equates the two codes. The equating process must occur before the comparisons for the matching are made.

Once equivalent record codes have been created for the two files, the comparison process can be implemented. Two different strategies have been used for the matching process. The first strategy involves sorting and ordering the two files by the identification numbers. Then, the two files are combined, and successive comparisons are made in order to identify matches. The second strategy involves selecting an element from one data base and comparing its identification number with identification numbers in the second file until either a match is achieved or the second file is exhausted. The SAS package has good subroutines for the matching process.

Data-Aggregation Techniques. Data-aggregation techniques are usually straightforward. In the case of continuous variables, subunits are averaged. In the case of categorical variables, two modes of aggregation are used. If the variables can be interpreted to assume values that can be placed in a linear scale, medians can be used for aggregation. If the variables fail to meet the linearity assumption, then the new unit is coded by the characteristics of a majority of the subunits or by subunit proportions.

In the data aggregation of continuous variables, potential ecological inferences must be identified. A correlation between subunit means and standard deviations can provide the needed information about variance loss due to aggregation. Cross tabulations provide the analogue for categorical variables. If the correlation is not large, then variance loss is present, and aggregation should be avoided. Burstein and others (1978) provide an excellent discussion of this problem. A second concern is the evenness and adequacy of representation of the new unit or upper-level unit by the subunits. Cross tabulations allow this concern to be investigated.

File-Modification Techniques. Most of the statistical packages contain a range of programming options for file modification. These options include routines to recode data, to conduct arithmetic operations, to make Boolean selections and establish conditional relationships, to add or delete variables, to sort and reorder files, and to exchange columns and rows. The file modification most frequently required in file preparation is a change in the level of the unit of organization. This process involves the exchange of columns and rows, the aggregation of data, the addition and deletion of variables, and the reorganization of records. After each file modification, the data base should be checked to see whether the operation was completed accurately.

Variable-Construction Techniques. There are several methods for the construction of variables. None appears to be error-free, and none can be used in all situations. Most composite variables represent a compromise between reliability and discrimination. This compromise often limits the composite variables, so that they only partially represent the surrogate measures for which they were constructed. Current methods for the construction of composite variables follow one of two basic strategies. One strategy adheres strictly to the hypothesized dimensionality of the composite variable. This strategy is based on a conceptual tie to theory or to research results reported in the literature. Methods employing this strategy include regression-scaled composite variables generated from theoretically formulated explicit measurement models (Costner, 1969; Blalock, 1968), discriminant analysis (Tatsuoka, 1972), variable scaling (Torgerson, 1958), and recomposed questionnaire responses (Cline and others, 1980). The second strategy is based on observed interrelationships among the variables and maximization of reliability. This strategy includes variable composition using factor scores (Kim and Mueller, 1978), canonical-factor regression (Allen, 1974), and cluster analysis (Fortune and others, 1981).

48

Summary

This chapter has focused on file preparation, a task that discussions of secondary analysis often overlook. The preparation of data files for secondary analysis varies in its complexity and in the specific activities required. This variation depends on two things: the research requirements of the planned secondary analysis and the conditions and characteristics of the primary data bases. This chapter has described more than twelve different preparation processes, and seven of the associated pitfalls — sample skews, merger mortality, nonresponse noise, variant variables, aggregate anomalies, time tangles, and mechanical misuses — have been defined and discussed. These pitfalls are encountered in any of the six families of techniques required for file preparation: file verification, sample verification, file merger, data aggregation, file modification, and variable construction. The discussion of these techniques may have made the process look extremely difficult. While the difficulty of file preparation is not insurmountable, it should never be underestimated.

References

Allen, M. P. "Construction of Composite Measures by the Canonical-Factor Regression Method." In H. L. Costner (Ed.), *Sociological Methodology 1973–74.* San Francisco: Jossey-Bass, 1974.

Bartz, A. E. *Basic Descriptive Statistics for Education and the Behavioral Sciences.* Minneapolis: Burgess, 1971.

Blalock, H. M. "The Measurement Problem: A Gap Between the Languages of Theory and Research." In H. M. Blalock and A. B. Blalock (Eds.), *Methodology in Social Research.* New York: McGraw-Hill, 1968.

Boruch, R. F. (Ed.). *Secondary Analysis.* New Directions for Program Evaluation, no. 4. San Francisco: Jossey-Bass, 1978.

Bryant, F. B., and Wortman, P. M. "Secondary Analysis: The Case for Data Archives." *American Psychologist,* 1978, *33,* 381–387.

Burstein, L., Linn, R. L., and Capell, F. J. "Analyzing Multilevel Data in the Presence of Heterogeneous Within-Class Regressions." *Journal of Educational Statistics,* 1978, *3,* 347–383.

Cline, M. G., Endahl, J. E., McBee, J. K., and Fortune, J. C. *Secondary Analysis of Headstart Transition Study: Final Report to Contract HEW–105–78–1303.* Washington, D.C.: U.S. Office of Education, 1980.

Cohen, J., and Cohen, P. *Applied Multiple Regression/Correlation Analysis for the Behavioral Sciences.* Hillsdale, N.J.: Erlbaum, 1975.

Cook, T. D., and Campbell, D. T. *Quasi-Experimentation: Design and Analysis Issues for Field Settings.* Chicago: Rand McNally, 1979.

Costner, H. L. "Theory, Deduction, and Rules of Correspondence." *American Journal of Sociology,* 1969, *75,* 245–263.

Dixon, W. J., and Brown, M. B. (Eds.). *BMDP-79.* Los Angeles: University of California Press, 1979.

Douglas, J. D. *Investigative Social Research.* Beverly Hills, Calif.: Sage, 1976.

Fortune, J. C., Endahl, J. E., McBee, J. K., Schultz, L. J., and Blecharczyk, S. R. "Comparison of Cluster Analysis Algorithms for Composite Variable Construction." Paper presented at a conference of the Northeastern Educational Research Association, Ellenville, N.Y., October 1981.

Helwig, J. T., and Council, K. A. (Eds.). *SAS User's Guide.* Cary, N.C.: SAS Institute, 1979.

Hofeditz, C. A. *Computers and Data Processing Made Simple.* Garden City, N.Y.: Doubleday, 1979.

Kim, J. O., and Mueller, C. W. *Introduction to Factor Analysis.* Beverly Hills, Calif.: Sage, 1978.

Kish, L. *Survey Sampling.* New York: Wiley, 1965.

Nie, N. H., Hull, C. H., Jenkins, J. G., Steinbrenner, K., and Bent, D. H. *SPSS.* New York: McGraw-Hill, 1975.

Sowell, E. J., and Casey, R. J. *Analyzing Educational Research.* Belmont, Calif.: Wadsworth, 1982.

Tatsuoka, M. M. *Multivariate Analysis: Techniques for Educational and Psychological Research.* New York: Wiley, 1972.

Torgerson, W. *The Theory and Methods of Scaling.* New York: Wiley, 1958.

Tukey, J. W. *Exploratory Data Analysis.* Reading, Mass.: Addison-Wesley, 1977.

Jim C. Fortune is professor of educational research and evaluation at Virginia Polytechnic Institute and State University, Blacksburg.

Janice K. McBee is research associate at Virginia Polytechnic Institute and State University, Blacksburg.

Once a data base that appears suitable is located, considerable work must still be done to make it ready for analysis. In particular, one must learn as much as possible about the data elements. To illustrate the importance of this point, the HEGIS data base and its uses are discussed in detail.

Using the Higher Education General Information Survey

Loyd D. Andrew

Every year, the National Center for Education Statistics (NCES) collects statistics from more than 3,000 institutions of higher education on enrollment, degrees awarded, finances, faculty salaries, and other matters. At less regular intervals, it collects statistics on facilities, libraries, and all employees. This data base, the Higher Education General Information Survey (HEGIS), is often maligned. It is hard to say why. Data bases, statistics, and statisticians are all criticized by those who need data in order to sell a program and by those who find the statistics threatening to funding requests. Not even the U.S. Bureau of the Census has escaped the wrath of those who found its most recent findings contrary to their city's interests. However, the nation is becoming increasingly dependent on statistics for policy analysis and decision making. For the policy analysts and decision makers in higher education, HEGIS is the richest resource. Nevertheless, it is still underused, probably due to some unfortunate incidents early in its life, to the complexity of higher education, and to ignorance of its strengths and weaknesses.

     The NCES uses data from HEGIS in preparing its annual report, *The Condition of Education,* several statistical reports, and in

D. J. Bowering (Ed.). *Secondary Analysis of Available Data Bases.* New Directions for Program Evaluation, no. 22. San Francisco: Jossey-Bass, June 1984.

newsletters, and statistics from HEGIS are used by the editors of the *Statistical Abstract of the United States* (U.S. Bureau of the Census). HEGIS data were used in more than 30 percent of the books on higher education published during the 1970s, and the popular media regularly use its data to report on faculty salaries, tuition, enrollments, and degrees awarded (Andrew and others, 1980). HEGIS statistics are used regularly by such educational associations as the American Council on Education, the American Association of Community and Junior Colleges, and the American Association of University Professors to assess the condition of various sectors and elements of higher education, including salaries in higher education and such issues as the progress of women in gaining equitable positions (Van Alystyne and others, 1977). These data are also used by such government agencies as the Bureau of Labor Statistics and the National Occupational Information Coordinating Committee in their manpower analyses and planning.

Despite these uses, institutional researchers concerned with the position of their institution relative to peer institutions and academic researchers and policy analysts still seem loathe to exploit the HEGIS data base to the fullest. For that reason, this chapter explains some of the uses to which HEGIS has been put, and it shows how HEGIS can be used to illuminate some of the issues concerning higher education. Too often, surveys are initiated to gather data that the NCES, other agencies of the federal government, and education associations have already collected. A better understanding of what is in HEGIS, how it has been used, and how it can be used may reduce the number of one-time and generally limited surveys that burden both researchers and respondents.

There are several reasons why the HEGIS data base is not being exploited as fully as it might be by those charged with policy and other research about higher education. In the late 1960s and early 1970s researchers were disappointed by delays between the collection and release of data, the accuracy of the data, and the poor documentation that accompanied computer tapes.

Timeliness is still a problem, but it is probably not as much of a problem as it is made out to be. Survey data generally become available on computer tapes between nine months and one year after they have been collected. While this delay may seem to be long, higher education institutions and their financial status appear to be reasonably stable. Unfortunately, neither the NCES nor others have systematically examined the stability of the data that are collected.

Currently, the data are probably sufficiently accurate to allow most institutional and policy questions to be answered. It is likely that many of the present perceptions about the accuracy of HEGIS are as much the fault of weak research designs as of the data themselves. There is still a tendency to overrate computer printout, particularly if the statistical analysis is complex. Computer output is only as good as the input, which means that its quality varies with the design and the definition of populations. Higher education is extremely diverse. Computer-generated statistical analyses make it easy to compare unlike segments of the population, unlike either in reality or as a result of differences in reporting.

Documentation for the computer tapes is reasonably good. However, the data base is still input- rather than output-oriented, which means that fairly large computer systems and relatively sophisticated data management programs are required if the data base is to be used effectively.

Development of the HEGIS Data Base

Precursors of the National Center for Education Statistics began to collect statistics about education in the middle of the nineteenth century. However, their data gathering, analysis, and use have not matched the sophistication of Bureau of the Census and Bureau of Labor Statistics efforts. The lag in data collection is pointed up by the special studies that Congress occasionally commissioned. For example, in 1932 Congress appropriated $200,000 for a study to determine the educational level of the American public.

In 1965, the National Center for Education Statistics formulated a comprehensive plan for the systematic collection of data about higher education, the character of which had changed enormously over ten years. In 1955, total full-time enrollment was 2.1 million; by 1965, it had more than doubled to 4.4 million. The relative share of enrollment in private education had declined from 45 percent of the market in 1955 to about 38 percent in 1965, although the number of students in both sectors had increased (Harris, 1972). During that decade, expenditures for education as a percentage of gross national product increased from 4.2 percent in 1955 to 6.6 percent in 1965. They reached a peak of 8 percent in 1975, and by 1979 they had declined to 7 percent (NCES, 1980).

During the 1960s, both public and private higher education struggled to keep up—in some cases to catch up—with demands for education. Funding for scholarships, buildings, and faculty was plentiful from both state and federal sources. However, higher education's management systems were unable to cope with the demand for education, the new influx of resources, and the rising tide of student and public concern about the missions and processes of higher education, and the institutions themselves were ill-prepared to complete the complex survey forms requesting information on enrollment, finances, degrees and awards, facilities, and libraries that NCES began to distribute in 1966–67. Counting and accounting practices varied from state to state and among institutions within individual states. Automated data processing of student and personnel records and to some degree of finance was nonexistent in small institutions and in its infancy even in larger institutions. Not until 1973 were financial definitions and data structures coordinated among the American Institute of Certified Public Accountants' audits of colleges and universities, the National Association of College and University Business Officers' administrative service, and the National Center for Higher Education Management Systems' higher education finance manual (Hyatt and Dickmeyer, 1980).

The National Center for Education Statistics itself appears to have been as poorly equipped as the institutions were to handle the multipage questionnaires completed by colleges and universities. Edits in those early days were nearly nonexistent, and program and tape documentation was minimal. It was difficult to order tapes, and it was even more difficult to find someone within the NCES who could answer questions. Use of these first data was also confounded by the lack of good data base management software, which at the time was still mostly a gleam in the eyes of software designers. Neither software nor hardware had become user-friendly.

Thus, it is not surprising that the first efforts of institutions and the NCES with the surveys of 1966–67 and several years thereafter were not altogether successful. However, the first surveys did allow a statistical portrait of higher education to be drawn (Harris, 1972). That comprehensive work used HEGIS data, earlier statistics on education, and data from such sources as the Bureau of the Census, the National Science Foundation, the Organization for Economic Cooperation and Development, and several education associations. The work was funded and supported by the Carnegie Commission on Higher Education. The effort required to draw data from the 1966–67 and 1967–68 surveys is still remembered with some anguish by programmers and analysts who worked at the University of California's Center of Higher Education (Foster, 1979). The resulting portrait covers student characteristics; population and educational attainment of the people of the United States; faculty characteristics, including supply and demand, outside earnings, and allocation of time; and institutions' income and expenditures, libraries and facilities, and enrollments.

No such comprehensive report exists on the characteristics of higher education today, although the enterprise is facing a revolution as radical as that of the sixties, albeit of a different sort. Research and teaching are becoming increasingly complex, and markets are changing. The faculty is unbalanced by age, tenure, sex, ethnicity, and knowledge of new technologies. Facilities and equipments are probably more obsolete than either the public or their users perceive them to be. Competition from other sectors of the economy is increasing. Finally, both the demand and the need for continuing education are probably underestimated.

In the early 1970s, such researchers as Cheit (1971) and Jellema (1973) began to use financial ratios to examine the condition of private higher education. Both authors were pessimistic about the viability of many private institutions of higher education, because the price position of these institutions was noncompetitive and because enrollments were projected to decline. This pessimism proved to be premature — perhaps because of these early warnings. In 1972, the federal government increased its support to both sectors of higher education with Basic Equal Opportunity Grants (now called Pell grants) and government-supported student loans. Since that time, many researchers have used the financial ratios developed by Cheit (1971), Jellema (1973), and others to study the viability of higher education institutions. These new studies generally draw data from HEGIS. In contrast, Cheit and Jellema conducted their own surveys. Perhaps they did not trust the HEGIS data for those early years, or they found them too expensive and difficult to extract from computer files, or they were too impatient to wait for the NCES to circulate the HEGIS data.

The National Commission on the Financing of Postsecondary Education was the next organization to make major use of the HEGIS. Its job was to develop policy recommendations for the funding of higher education. The Commission came into being as a result of Congress's frustration with the lack of information that could be used to develop a policy in that area (Gladieux and Wolanin, 1976). The impact of the Commission's work on federal policy is difficult to document. However, there appears to be little question about the effect on federal, state, and institutional decisions of the series of studies commissioned by the Carnegie Commission on Higher Education and of the first and second Newman reports (Newman, 1971, 1973). Less driven by numbers than the massive work of the national commission, these studies and reports used case studies and observation as well as statistics. The writers, who often worked in teams, assessed, critiqued, and recommended directions for higher education. In general, the statistics used in their reports came not from computer tapes but from NCES publications. These documents are published with reasonable timeliness and regularity. The same cannot be said, particularly in recent years, for other NCES summaries of the HEGIS data, for example, Financial Statistics of Institutions of Higher Education, Current Funds Revenues and Expenditures, and Fall Enrollment in Higher Education.

Few national studies used HEGIS computer files after the National Commission on the Financing of Postsecondary Education completed its work in 1972 until 1976, when Andrew and Friedman (1976), Van Alstyne and Coldren (1976), and Lupton and others (1976) almost simultaneously merged data from many different HEGIS computer files to construct sets of financial ratios for analyzing the financial condition of various sectors and regions of higher education. Andrew and Friedman (1976) attempted to determine whether financial indicators could be used to predict the demise of small liberal arts colleges. Lupton and others (1976) used many of the same financial ratios with Bureau of the Census data to project a somewhat gloomy picture of declining enrollments and worsening economic conditions for many sectors and regions of higher education. Van Alstyne and Coldren (1976) initiated what became a long-term project to test the use of financial indicators in the measurement of institutional viability.

In his summary of work on indicators of financial conditions, Collier (1979) underscored the problem of defining financial stress or health. He suggested that there were four useful indicators of stress: working capital distress, demand-related revenue distress, non-sales-related revenue distress, and financial flexibility distress. Obviously, the strategies used to cope with stress, either locally or nationally, depend on the type of stress. Case studies by Andrew and Friedman (1976) and by the Financial Assessment project (Hyatt and Dickmeyer, 1980) indicated that both internal and external factors were important in determining institutional viablity and resistance to or recovery from distress. The workbook by Dickmeyer and Hughes (1980) was one valuable by-product of the Financial Assessment project.

After 1976, the volume of studies using merged data from HEGIS increased rapidly. Farmer (1977) used the data to examine the financial health of independent colleges and universities in New York state. St. John and others (1977) used HEGIS, OCR, and Title III data bases to perform a descriptive analysis of institutional change. Jackson (1977) described merged data bases, and McCoy and Halstead (1979) studied higher education financing in the fifty states. Variations in organizational and funding structures among states and institutions and their effects on financial reporting produced some unanticipated and unwelcome results. In a later study, McCoy and Halstead (1982) conquered some of the problems created by variances in reporting. For example, in some states, the costs of medical centers are referred to the institutions with which they are associated; in other states, this is not so. Many of the differences among states in the reporting of expenditures and other statistics are uncovered only as the data base is used and as cries of anguish about findings are heard. State and institutional administrators are highly sensitive to cost comparisons. Their reactions to what they perceive as inappropriate or wrong comparisons often obscure the overall merit of a given study and of the data base on which it is based. They are less sensitive to studies about the total condition of higher education and about trends in conditions. The most notable and consistent of these types of studies are by Minter and Bowen (Bowen, 1980; Minter and Bowen, 1975, 1976, 1977, 1978, 1980, 1982) on the condition of higher education.

The power of the HEGIS data base for other kinds of analysis is demonstrated by the materials in Andrew and others (1982).

A Description of HEGIS

This section describes each of the major HEGIS surveys. For a full understanding of these surveys, it is best to examine the survey questionnaires, which can be obtained from the NCES. Since the data base is no more perfect than the other works of women and men—and some 10,000 women and men participate in the building of HEGIS— the descriptions that follow include some caveats. All the surveys have three data elements in common: a FICE code identifying the institution, names and addresses, and definitions of data elements. The FICE code is the common link between surveys that allows data from different files to be merged. The names and addresses include those of the institution and the institutional respondent and a code identifying the respondent entity as a whole institution, branch, campus, or some other organizational unit. Definitions of data elements posed a problem for early HEGIS surveys. Respondents seemed either not to read them or not to interpret them consistently. This problem has become less acute as increasing numbers of institutions have programmed their own data processors to answer HEGIS questions. However, interpretation poses a problem for researchers when they first use the data base. Moreover, some definitions have changed over time. Thus, researchers who conduct longitudinal studies must sometimes make adjustments. The most recent change—redesign of the instructional program taxonomy in 1981 — was fairly substantial. A new redesign effort of even greater magnitude has just been started. This effort has been undertaken to reduce the respondents' burden and to eliminate the double counting of certain types of students because data on these students were being collected by three different surveys — the HEGIS, the Vocational Education Data Survey, and the Noncollegiate Survey. The redesign will collapse these three surveys into a single survey, which will be known as the Integrated Postsecondary Data System (IPEDS). The redesign will develop a cross-walk among the new and post surveys to protect users who wish to do longitudinal studies. Despite the NCES's sensitivity to concerns expressed both by respondents and by users about the stability of questionnaires from year to year, the new survey will probably encounter some problems in maintaining consistency of data element definitions and developing cross-walk procedures, at least in the first years.

Financial Surveys. Data from the financial survey have seen the most extensive use and testing of all the surveys, because of the emphasis among policy analysts and researchers on the financial status of institutions and of the enterprise as a whole. As a result, more is known about the problems with this data set than about the problems of others. The survey instrument is relatively short — four pages long. It has seven parts.

Part A collects information on current funds revenues by source for the fiscal year. There are six major sources of revenue: tuition and fees; government appropriations; government contracts and grants; private gifts, grants, and contracts; endowment income; and sales and services of two types — other sources and independent operations. Researchers who wish to merge data from the enrollment and financial surveys to determine cost or revenues per student should use enrollment data from fall of the year previous to the fiscal year under examination. For example, fall 1982 enrollments should be used with fiscal year 1983 financial data to compute the ratio of costs per student. Differences in how institutions complete Part A have created two problems. First, institutions differ in their reporting of tuition and fees. In some states, tuition and fees are treated as offsets against state appropriations. In others, they go directly into the state's general revenue. The NCES has been urged to ask respondents to note the practice followed and to include caveats in the data bases themselves. At last report, these procedures have not been instituted. Second, states also differ in the way in which they process government appropriations. Thus, researchers who wish to make interstate comparisons should determine what is included in federal, state, and local appropriations so that appropriate adjustments can be made. As already noted, some institutions include expenditures for related organizations in their cost report, and other institutions do not.

Part B collects information about current funds expenditures and mandatory transfers for the fiscal year. Part B collects this information under four major headings. Nine programs are included under educational and general expenditures: instruction, research, public service, academic support, student services, institutional support, operation and maintenance of plant, institutionally funded scholarships and fellowships, and educational and general mandatory transfers. Expenditures of these types are totaled. Data for these nine line items and the total have probably been used more often in the national assessments than any other data collection in the financial survey. Part B also includes expenditures for auxiliary enterprises, hospitals, and independent operations.

Part C collects information on physical plant assets — beginning and end book values of land, buildings, and equipments and the replacement value of buildings. Few researchers have used these data. My own experience with the information collected by Parts C and D has not been encouraging.

Part D collects information on indebtedness on physical plant. As such, it should provide reasonably good information that could be used to determine the indebtedness of private institutions for physical plant and of public institutions for their auxiliaries' physical plant. Moreover, as creative financing becomes more popular among public institutions, this section may become more useful in studying public institutions' indebtedness. However, the instructions and definitions may have to be revised in order to pick up the practice that borrows against endowments and projected appropriations to compensate for shortfalls in state appropriations.

The questions in Part E concern book and market value and yields of the institution's endowment assets. Part F is a statement of changes in fund balances for the fiscal year. The questions collect information on unrestricted and restricted current funds, loan funds, endowment funds, annuity and life income funds, and plant funds. Part G is for public institutions only. It includes questions on revenues, expenditures, debts, cash, and security holdings. Part G was included at the request of the Bureau of the Census.

Fall Enrollment Survey. The fall enrollment survey has two sections: one for four-year institutions and one for two-year colleges. The questions in each section are approximately the same. The questions collect information on enrollments of full- and part-time students by six ethnic groups and the two sexes. For the senior institutions, full-time students are broken out by the following groups: undergraduates (first-time freshmen, other, first-year, second-year, third-year, fourth-year, and beyond), unclassified students (undergraduate and postbaccalaureate), first professionals, and graduates (first-time graduate students and all other graduate students). Similar information is sought on part-time students. The two-year college survey seeks information on first-time freshmen, all other undergraduates, and unclassified students. Until 1977, the fall enrollment survey also collected information by field. Data from files for 1977 and prior years are useful for estimating attrition by field when used in conjunction with files on degrees conferred.

No major difficulties in using enrollment survey data have been reported. A field audit of a sample of schools found a less than 1 percent discrepancy between audited enrollments and HEGIS-reported enrollments (Westat, 1979). Collection of racial and ethnic data poses some problems, because the manner of collection has been left to the individual institutions. Moreover, some students resent giving information on ethnic membership and either refuse to report it or report it wrongly. Different schools estimate for student nonresponses in different ways. The error is probably negligible. Finally, some ethnic groups believe that the HEGIS classification of ethnic groups is inadequate, arguing that the HEGIS system does not make it possible to assess progress in meeting goals of equal opportunity. Computation of full-time equivalence may pose a small problem. Instructions on the data collection instrument suggest that the institution should use its own method and data. Since institutions differ in this respect, the instructions probably create some small discrepancies.

Residence and Migration of College Students. The residence and migration of college students survey is used mostly by state agencies of higher education, which are concerned about the migration of students. With this questionnaire, the NCES attempts to discover where first-time students come from. The statistics are used, so the data base must have some credibility. However, differences in tuition for in-state and out-of-state students give students a strong incentive to establish residency before enrolling.

Degrees and Other Formal Awards Conferred. At fifty-one pages, this is the longest of the NCES's questionnaires. Institutions report the number of bachelor's, master's, and doctor's degrees awarded in twenty-four disciplines and in many more sub-disciplines. In education alone, there are thirty-four subdisciplines. In addition, data are collected on first professional degrees in selected fields. Two-year colleges report degrees and awards for occupational and academic fields. Degrees and awards are broken out for sex by subdisciplines and for ethnic group by major discipline. By itself, this survey is useful in performing analyses of changes in the mix of graduates by field, by sex, and by ethnicity. It can also be used with enrollments, particularly with the earlier enrollment surveys, which obtained data by field for the purpose of estimating attrition. There have been few complaints about the accuracy of this survey's data.

Salaries, Tenure, and Fringe Benefits Survey. The American Association of University Professors uses data from the NCES survey on salaries, tenure, and fringe benefits for its annual report on the status of faculty. The survey seeks data on the number of faculty, total salary outlay, and the number of tenured faculty by sex and for six different ranks, from professor through no academic rank, for both nine- and twelve-month faculty. In addition, it gathers data on expenditures and number of faculty covered for eleven types of fringe benefits.

Data from the survey probably understate faculty salary, for despite instructions to the contrary, it seems likely that some institutions count nine-month faculty who receive salaries over twelve months as twelve-month faculty. In addition, salary data are not collected on nine-month faculty who work on summer contracts. Moreover, no data are collected on consulting fees or on consulting day benefits. However, the most serious difficulty with this survey may be that no data are collected on part-time faculty, who provide much of the instructional support in many colleges, in particular in community colleges and the less traditional types of schools. Thus, the data on numbers and salaries should not be used to compute total faculty costs. Also, ranks at different schools are not always comparable; for example, Harvard rankings start with associate professor.

Employees. At less frequent intervals, the NCES also collects data on employees other than faculty. This survey generally seeks information on administrators' salaries and on the number of personnel in such occupations or programs as instruction, administration, technical, maintenance, skilled crafts, secretarial, and professional nonfaculty. Again, data are broken out by race and sex. Data from this survey have not been used as much as faculty data to study the effects of affirmative action policies or other matters. However, as competition for certain occupational skills increases and as cost-effectiveness receives more attention, information from this survey may see more use.

Facilities and Libraries. At irregular intervals, the NCES has used separate surveys to collect data on facilities and libraries. The library questionnaire is not generally considered to be very good by librarians, who consider surveys by their own associations to be more useful. The facilities survey could provide useful information for policy and funding decisions at the national level, particularly now that equipment and, to some degree, buildings rapidly are becoming obsolescent. However, the survey is not sensitive to technological obsolescence, as its questions are limited to type of space and equipment by condition and of utilization. Information is also sought on acreage and library size, holdings, expenditures, and staff.

Institutional Characteristics Survey. The institutional characteristics survey is the key to all the surveys. The directory compiled from the information that it gathers describes colleges and universities by FICE code number, corporate name, address, telephone number, congressional district, number and addresses of branch campuses, sources and types of accreditation for the institution and its educational programs, control, sex of student body, levels of educational work, numbers of students, and minimum admission requirements. At one time, the survey also collected the names and telephone numbers of the institutions' principal officers, which made the resulting directory an excellent source of information. Unlike most of the other summaries resulting from the HEGIS surveys, the Directory of Institutions of Higher Education is published reasonably soon after the data are collected.

Using HEGIS in Research

This section has two parts. The first part describes some of the ratios that have been developed for the study of higher education, and it discusses some of the recent research. The second part recommends some procedures for using HEGIS computer files.

Useful Ratios. Until the 1970s, higher education was generally described by enrollments, earned degrees, and expenditures. Very little systematic analysis using statistical data was involved in the making or assessment of policy and strategies. *The Condition of Higher Education* represents this tradition. A collection of statistics, it describes the condition and provides a base for policy analysis. It does not assess conditions or recommend what could be done to change conditions. These tasks are left to others. Many have accepted the challenge. Yet, despite some very serious and important work in the seventies, policy analysis is still in its infancy as far as techniques are concerned, although it has borrowed heavily from other fields.

In general, both evaluation and the development of policy

recommendations require the merging of data from many different HEGIS files with data from other sources, such as the National Science Foundation, the Bureau of Labor Statistics, and the Bureau of the Census. Some of the ratios that have been used to assess the condition of higher education include costs per student (the ratio between expenditures in two programs such as the ratio between administration and instruction, or between program expenditures and total expenditures), estimates of attrition (by discipline, if enrollment data from years prior to 1977 are used), trends in enrollment and degrees awarded, and trends in costs by programs.

There are others, of course. In studying the costs of higher education, Bowen (1980) used the following: percent distribution of current educational expenditures by eight categories; teaching, student services, scholarships and fellowships, academic support, institutional support, operation and maintenance of plant, mandatory transfers, and others; percent distribution of current educational expenditures by categories of clientele or recipients, such as faculty (compensation), other staff (compensation), vendors of goods and services (purchases), and students (scholarships and fellowships); campus building space per student unit, expenditures for additions to physical plant as percentage of total educational and general expenditures; building space assigned to classroom as percentage of total building space; and average endowment at market value per student unit. As noted earlier, faculty salary data do not include part-time faculty; therefore, it is likely that faculty compensation will be understated when expenditures are computed by type of expense.

Andrew and Friedman (1976) as well as others have used the following ratios: current fund expenditures to current fund revenues (not very illuminating, for colleges tend to spend what they get); auxiliary expenditures to auxiliary revenues; the various sources of revenue as a percent of total revenues; and the sources of revenue per full-time student. The sources of revenue were outlined earlier in this chapter when the data base was described. This set of ratios, along with size, control, and some of the ratios of expenditures, can be used with cluster analysis to classify institutions. About the only source of revenue that some analysts would not include when calculating revenue per full-time student is revenue for grants and contracts per student. However, the ratio is useful. While most grants and contracts are for research, not instruction or student support, these programs often derive benefits from such funding. One problem with most accounting practices and in particular with fund accounting is that they obscure joint benefits and costs. Research grants and contracts, as well as faculty consulting, which shows up nowhere on the books as either a cost or a benefit, should be treated as a joint, if hidden, benefit to instructional programs, since they generally contribute to faculty development and to acquisition of equipment, and they often provide scholarships for students.

Dickmeyer and Hughes (1980) provide a useful set of statistics for planning and evaluation at the institutional level. Some of the statistics that they suggest for trend analysis are also useful in classifying institutions: total enrollment by program, total degrees, degrees by level and program, total expenditures, and revenues by source. Trend analysis using institutional data alone can provide considerable insights when developing strategies to prevent or alleviate distress. However, decision making is usually enriched by comparisons with competitive or similar institutions. Such analyses generally require the use of HEGIS or other data bases.

Hyer (1982) used data from the HEGIS faculty salary survey to follow up on earlier works on the status of women in higher education. She selected four variables: change in the proportion of women on the faculty, change in the ratio of men to women faculty, change in the number of full-time female professors, and change in the number of tenured female faculty. From her analyses of data from the 1974 and 1980 faculty salary surveys, she determined that the proportion of women on teaching faculties in doctorate-granting universities had increased—mostly in the lower ranks. Waldenberg (1982) showed that the distribution of female recipients of baccalaureate degrees changed considerably between 1968 and 1980: In 1968, 37 percent of the female graduates received a degree in education; by 1980, this proportion had declined to 19 percent. Disciplines recording gains included business, the health professions, and engineering, and the representation of women in physics dropped.

A recent controversial study involving the use of HEGIS financial and enrollment data was conducted by Avent (1982), who analyzed revenues for selected black and white institutions of higher education. Using data from the financial and enrollment surveys for 1970-71, 1974-75, and 1978-79, he compared seven sources of revenue per student for black and white colleges matched by mission, control, size, and other factors. His trend analysis was not confounded by changes in the financial survey in the mid 1970s, since he used revenues rather than expenditures. He found no significant differences in the funding patterns for the matched colleges.

Malitz (1982) demonstrated the compatibility of HEGIS with other data files when he studied the response of public community colleges to labor market demand. He cross-walked data from HEGIS files on earned degrees and institutional characteristics to major occupational categories (National Occupational Information Coordinating Committee, 1978 and labor market projections, U.S. Bureau of Labor Statistics, 1976–77).

Several states make use of HEGIS data. For example, Nebraska uses data from the financial, enrollment, and degrees conferred surveys to create five-year benchmarks for major decisions. In addition, it uses actual numbers and percent distributions of fall headcount enrollments, degrees granted, education and general revenue, education and general expenditures, and full-time instructional faculty. Fuller (1982) recommends the use of five years of data for trend analysis. Such analysis is sometimes confounded by the inevitable changes in survey formats, questions, and instructions, the most recent of such changes being the new instructional taxonomy. However, this change did not create too many difficulties for Nebraska, since it uses major programs, as Fuller recommends.

Bowering (1982) used data from National Science Foundation surveys in combination with HEGIS data to address such questions as these: Does federally sponsored research and development have an effect on educational outcomes? Are models of potential effects different for different fields of science? Are they different for groups of private and public universities?

On the leading edge of efforts to use HEGIS data are the studies that seek to determine the effects of market and financial resources on institutional behavior. Considerable efforts have been made to use the data to assess and predict the financial health of individual institutions or groups of institutions, but the results have been somewhat mixed. A more ambitious undertaking has been to test the hypothesis that the level and mix of resources reflected in financial ratios and disciplines has an effect on how institutions respond to external forces. For example, Holmes and Andrew (1982) examined the impact of funding provided by the federal government to encourage training in the professional allied health field on the programs of black colleges. These authors used many of the ratios developed in past studies of financial condition to test institutional responsiveness. The results were inconclusive, but there were indications that the colleges in the sample were more likely to be responsive to market opportunities if they were neither too poor nor too rich.

Recommendations for Using the HEGIS Data Base. For those who have access to a reasonably large computer and a good data management and statistical software package, such as the Statistical

Analysis System (SAS), using HEGIS is remarkably simple. Indeed, it is almost too simple. This simplicity tempts the researcher to ask a few research questions, design an analytical procedure, and then leave it to the computer to crunch out some answers. The results are usually garbage — but not because the data in the files are garbage. The results are garbage because the researcher has not taken the steps that she or he would have had to take to design a survey form and develop a sample. Having to identify or create questions that fit the research problem and population forces the researcher to do a preliminary investigation of the population's language, location, and style or procedures. Generally, such surveys are pilot-tested, and questionnaires and analytical procedures are revised after the tests.

Too often, this basic discipline is abandoned when large, off-the-shelf data bases are used. Of course, the very size of the data base can be inhibiting. Perhaps we tender too much respect to the products of bureaucracies that have spent many years designing questions and logistic systems that purr away automatically, churning out questions and obtaining high response rates. Bureaucracies are very good at such things; they are also very prone to forget the original purposes of the procedures and processes that they developed. Generally, they are not very curious about what they do, and they are not very good at documentation. Those who collect data in bureaucracies often do not use it. To offset this, the NCES has regularly sponsored meetings with both users and suppliers of the data. However, such meetings are a poor substitute for hands-on manipulation of data.

Such manipulation, if it occurs, is done by researchers, and they do not always document what they encounter. Probably more has been learned about the problems with using HEGIS in the last four years than in the previous ten as a result of the research on financial indicators that the NCES and the education associations have sponsored. Unfortunately, what has been learned has not been shared to any great extent with the general population of users. While the proceedings of the conferences concerning the users of HEGIS for financial analysis are available through ERIC, neither the titles nor the descriptors make it clear that considerable information about using the data base is available in the documents. Furthermore, no publication can ever substitute for hands-on experience and sharing of experiences.

Probably the most common problem for those who use the data base for the first time lies in understanding its terms and instructions. They seem clear, but they are not. Before the researcher can understand these instructions and how they may have been interpreted, the researcher must know what lies behind them and the associated definitions and how they are implemented.

Thus, the first rule in using the HEGIS data base is this: Visit at least one and preferably several organizational units that complete the questionnaire, and find out how they do so — both by asking and, if possible, by observing. For example, before using the financial file, visit the finance officers at several institutions and find out what finance information they use to complete the HEGIS questionnaire.

Of course, before visiting any offices, the researcher should read the basic literature on their operations. For finance, the best sources are probably the publications of the National Association of College and University Business Officers. For each of the major university functions, there is a professional association that attempts to develop standard reporting procedures. Most of these associations also use HEGIS or similar data bases for their own research, so they are familiar with differences in reporting processes and with the data base itself. Talk to the researchers at these associations, and use their reports. An enormous amount of good information is developed by government agencies and associations. Much of this information is published in forms that escape the journals and card catalogues. The best way of finding this literature is by beginning with the research teams at the agencies and associations. As a follow-up, find a librarian who can lead you through government and association report-cataloguing systems. Do not limit your searches to the ERIC system. It is good, but it does not cover all the publications and reports. Some of the better writers in the field of higher education are underrepresented in ERIC and the journals that it indexes.

The next step follows from the diversity of mission, governance, size, operations, and funding among states and institutions. The objectives and problems of public and private institutions are quite different, and these differences are reflected in their financial reports. As noted earlier, public institutions may or may not be responsible for accounting for and expending fringe benefits. If they are not, they did not report these benefits to HEGIS in the past. To obtain such information, the NCES has instituted a "fix" outside of normal accounting procedures, and such fixes tend to get lost.

The effect of size is almost as important as the effect of governance and control on how institutions respond to questionnaires. Large private and public institutions tend to be much better staffed and equipped than small institutions for accounting and counting and for responding to questions. Their data are likely to be much more consistent than the data supplied by small institutions, in particular for institutions that operate at the margin. In addition, institutions with strong, centralized management will be more consistent in their reports, whether they are public or private. However, they are not always more accurate. This leads to the next rule: Discover everything that you can about the populations that you will be studying, and use this information in your design of data edits and analytical treatment. There are a few good books on state governance of higher education, and the researcher should read them. However, the best sources of information are probably the state higher education agencies, legislative analysts and budget offices, and enabling and appropriation acts. Never stop with your first source. Use several sources, and cross-check the information. Governance is ambiguous. Most of the groups just noted handle data regularly. Thus, they generally have a good understanding of what is in the data bases and of what to look out for.

The next step is to run a pilot test. There are more than three thousand colleges and universities in the HEGIS data base. Some complete all reports, while others do not. For example, Duke University does not complete the finance questionnaire. The amount of paper that can emerge from a computer for three thousand records in four or five surveys is enormous. Pull a random sample of the populations with which you will be working, and examine the data. Find out what is missing and why. If possible, check one year's report against reports from previous years. Develop some criteria for determining whether the data are reasonable. The costs per student of universities with and without medical schools are in the same range unless one school includes the costs of the medical school in its financial report and the other does not. Compute a standard set of descriptive statistics — means, modes, standard deviations. Look at the outliers, and find out why they are outliers. Use the telephone to test your guesses with those whom you cultivated in the first step.

The next procedures to be described resemble standard edit procedures. It can be assumed that you will not begin these procedures until you have defined your subpopulations, until you know the background of instructions, until you understand how data are recorded at the first level and how they are processed into the data base, and until you have established some working criteria or tolerances for testing the data.

The first step in an edit is to determine whether the records add up. Is there the same number of files as there are schools? What data are missing? For example, all schools do not offer all degrees, so open cells in the degree files do not necessarily mean that the school did not complete the report, nor do they mean that the school does not have a program; no one may have been graduated in the year at which you are looking.

The next step is to get a better or more strict definition of populations. The classified structure of HEGIS uses very broad categories to define colleges and universities. These categories are generally not fine enough for most research. Cluster analysis using some of the ratios developed by Korb and Huddleston (1982) is one means of describing groups of institutions more accurately.

Next, build some criteria into the computer process so that schools that do not meet them are rejected as exceptions. Then, run your data. You will want to develop your own criteria, but here are some rules of thumb: Look at all schools that are outside two standard deviations on a given ratio. There should not be many, because you have already used some key ratios to group your schools into relatively small clusters that have size, costs per student, proportionate shares of research grants and contracts and other sources of revenue, and proportionate distribution of expenditures among programs in common. Look at the schools that do not meet your criteria. If you follow the procedures just outlined to determine the average cost per student for the total universe, you will not have entered Duke University into your study. It is surely worth a footnote in your study that you have probably understated costs per student as a result, but the understatement is not nearly as large as it would have been if you had kept Duke's students but not its costs.

Conclusion

In the next ten years, policy analysis will become increasingly useful in setting goals and determining funding levels for higher education. Many institutions are going to have problems. There are substantial data bases that can be used to address the questions that will be raised, including questions involving higher education's responsiveness to changing societal conditions. In using these data bases, researchers must apply the same discipline that they would follow if they were collecting their own data.

References

Andrew, L., Cuthbert, A., and Nelson, L. (Eds.). *Research in Postsecondary Education: Utilization of HEGIS and Other National Data Bases.* Blacksburg: College of Education, Virginia Polytechnic Institution and State University, 1982.

Andrew, L., Fortune, J., and McCluskey, L. *Final Report: Analysis of Use of HEGIS Data.* Blacksburg: Virginia Polytechnic Institution and State University, 1981.

Andrew, L., and Friedman, B. *Demise of Certain Private Liberal Arts Colleges.* Blacksburg: College of Education, Virginia Polytechnic Institution and State University, 1976.

Avent, D. "Revenue Patterns for Selected Black and White Institutions of Higher Education." In L. Andrew, A. Cuthbert, and L. Nelson (Eds.), *Research in Post-*

secondary Education: Utilization of HEGIS and Other National Data Bases. Blacksburg: College of Education, Virginia Polytechnic Institution and State University, 1982.

Bowen, H. R. The Costs of Higher Education: How Much Do Colleges and Universities Spend Per Student and How Much Should They Spend? San Francisco: Jossey-Bass, 1980.

Bowering, D. "Assessing the Impact of Federally Sponsored R&D Expenditures in Science and Engineering on Leading Research Universities and Colleges." In. L. Andrew, A. Cuthbert, and L. Nelson (Eds.), Research in Postsecondary Education: Utilization of HEGIS and Other National Data Bases. Blacksburg: College of Education, Virgnia Polytechnic Institution and State University, 1982.

Bureau of the Census, U.S. Department of Commerce. Statistical Abstract of the United States. Washington, D.C.: U.S. Government Printing Office. Published annually.

Bureau of Labor Statistics, U.S. Department of Labor. Occupational Outlook Handbook, 1976-77. Washington, D.C.: Government Printing Office, 1976.

Cheit, E. F. The New Depression in Higher Education. New York: McGraw-Hill, 1971.

Collier, D. Assessing Financial Distress in Colleges and Universities. Boulder, Colo.: National Center for Higher Education Management Systems, 1979.

Dickmeyer, N., and Hughes, K. S. Financial Self-Assessment: A Workbook for Colleges. Washington, D.C.: National Association of College and University Business Officers, 1980.

Farmer, J. Financial Health of Independent Colleges and Universities in New York. Albany, N.Y.: Temporary State Commission on the Future of Postsecondary Education, 1977.

Foster, P. Personal communications, 1979.

Fuller, W. S. "Indexing with HEGIS." In L. Andrew, A. Cuthbert, and L. Nelson (Eds.), Research in Postsecondary Education: Utilization of HEGIS and Other National Data Bases. Blacksburg: College of Education, Virginia Polytechnic Institute and State University, 1982.

Gladieux, L. E., and Wolanin, T. R. Congress and the Colleges. Lexington, Mass.: Heath, 1976.

Harris, S. A Statistical Portrait of Higher Education. New York: McGraw-Hill, 1972.

Holmes, E., and Andrew, L. "Operating Ratios and Institutional Characteristics Affecting the Responsiveness of Black Colleges and Universities to Professional Allied Health Programs." In L. Andrew, A. Cuthbert, and L. Nelson (Eds.), Research in Postsecondary Education: Utilization of HEGIS and Other National Data Bases. Blacksburg: College of Education, Virginia Polytechnic University and State University, 1982.

Hyatt, J., and Dickmeyer, N. (Eds.). Proceedings of the Joint Study Group on the Utility of HEGIS Finance Data: An Analysis of the Utility of HEGIS Financial Data in Conducting Institutional and Higher Education Sector Comparisons. Washington, D.C.: National Association of College and University Business Officers, 1980. (ED 191 415)

Hyer, P. "Affirmative Action for Women: An Assessment of Progress at Doctorate-Granting Universities." In L. Andrew, A. Cuthbert, and L. Nelson (Eds.), Research in Postsecondary Education: Utilization of HEGIS and Other National Data Bases. Blacksburg: College of Education, Virginia Polytechnic Institute and State University, 1982.

Jackson, G. A. "Appendix F: Description of Merged Data Bases." In G. Weathersby and others, Final Report: The Development of Institutions of Higher Education: Theory and Assessment of Impact of Four Possible Areas of Federal Intervention. Cambridge, Mass.: Harvard School of Education, 1977.

Jellema, W. W. From Red to Black? San Francisco: Jossey-Bass, 1973.

Korb, R., and Huddleston, E. "Clusters of Colleges and Universities: An Empirically Determined System." Paper presented at annual meeting of the American Educational Research Association, New York, 1982.

71

Lupton, A., Augenblick, J., and Heyison, J. "The Financial State of Higher Education." *Change,* 1976, *8* (8), 21–35.

McCoy, M., and Halstead, K. *Higher Education Financing in the Fifty States: Interstate Comparisons, Fiscal Year 1976.* Boulder, Colo.: National Center for Higher Education Management Systems, 1979.

McCoy, M., and Halstead, K. *Higher Education Financing in the Fifty States: Interstate Comparisons, Fiscal Year 1979.* (2nd ed.) Boulder, Colo.: National Center for Higher Education Management Systems, 1982.

Malitz, G. "Public Two-Year Colleges Response to Labor Market Projects in the 1970s." In L. Andrew, A. Cuthbert, and L. Nelson (Eds.), *Research in Postsecondary Education: Utilization of HEGIS and Other National Data Bases.* Blacksburg: College of Education, Virginia Polytechnic Institute and State University, 1982.

Minter, W. J., and Bowen, H. R. *Independent Higher Education: First Annual Report on Financial and Educational Trends in Independent Sector of American Higher Education.* Washington, D.C.: National Association of Independent Colleges and Universities, 1975. (ED 119 570)

Minter, W. J., and Bowen, H. R. *Independent Higher Education: Second Annual Report on Financial and Educational Trends in Independent Sector of American Higher Education.* Washington, D.C.: National Association of Independent Colleges and Universities, 1976. (ED 127 844)

Minter, W. J., and Bowen, H. R. *Independent Higher Education: Third Annual Report on Financial and Educational Trends in Independent Sector of American Higher Education.* Washington, D.C.: National Association of Independent Colleges and Universities, 1977. (ED 145 793)

Minter, W. J., and Bowen, H. R. *Independent Higher Education: Fourth Annual Report on Financial and Educational Trends in Independent Sector of American Higher Education.* Washington, D.C.: National Association of Independent Colleges and Universities, 1978. (ED 158 653)

Minter, W. J., and Bowen, H. R. *Independent Higher Education: Fifth Annual Report on Financial and Educational Trends in Independent Sector of American Higher Education.* Washington, D.C.: National Association of Independent Colleges and Universities, 1980. (ED 189 994)

Minter, J., and Bowen, H. "The Minter-Bowen Report." *The Chronicle of Higher Education,* 1982, *24* (11), *24* (12), *24* (13), *24* (14).

National Center for Education Statistics. *The Condition of Higher Education.* Washington, D.C.: U.S. Government Printing Office. Published annually.

National Center for Education Statistics. *Digest of Education Statistics.* Washington, D.C.: U.S. Government Printing Office, 1980.

National Center for Education Statistics. *Projections of Education Statistics to 1990–91.* Washington, D.C.: U.S. Government Printing Office.

National Center for Education Statistics. *HEGIS: Financial Statistics of Institutions of Higher Education.* Washington, D.C.: U.S. Government Printing Office.

National Center for Education Statistics. *Current Funds Revenues and Expenditures.* Washington, D.C.: U.S. Government Printing Office.

National Center for Education Statistics. *Fall Enrollment in Higher Education.* Washington, D.C.: U.S. Government Printing Office.

National Commission on the Financing of Postsecondary Education. *Financing Postsecondary Education in the United States.* Washington, D.C.: U.S. Government Printing Office, 1973.

National Occupational Information Coordinating Committee. *Vocational Preparation and Occupations.* Washington, D.C.: U.S. Government Printing Office, 1978.

Newman, F. *Report on Higher Education.* Washington, D.C.: U.S. Department of Health, Education, and Welfare, 1971.

72

Newman, F. *The Second Newman Report: National Policy and Higher Education.* Cambridge, Mass.: M.I.T. Press, 1973.

St. John, E. P., Tingley, T., and Gallos, J. "Appendix C: Descriptive Analysis of Institutional Change Using HEGIS, CFAE, OCR, and Title III Data Bases." In G. Weathersby and others, *Final Report: The Development of Institutions of Higher Education: Theory and Assessment of Impact of Four Possible Areas of Federal Intervention.* Cambridge, Mass.: Harvard School of Education, 1977.

Van Alstyne, C., and Coldren, S. L. *The Financial Measures Project: Development and Application of Measures of Financial Conditions of Colleges and Universities.* Washington, D.C.: American Council on Education, 1976.

Van Alstyne, C., Withers, J. S., and Elliott, S. A. "Affirmative Inaction: The Bottom Line Tells the Tale." *Change,* 1977, *9* (8), 39–41, 60.

Westat. *Postsurvey Validation of Fall Enrollment in Institutions of Higher Education.* Washington, D.C.: National Center for Education Statistics, 1979.

Waldenberg, A. "Female Representation Among Baccalaureate Degree Recipients: Retrospect and Prospect." In L. Andrew, A. Cuthbert, and L. Nelson (Eds.), *Research in Postsecondary Education: Utilization of HEGIS and Other National Data Bases.* Blacksburg: College of Education, Virginia Polytechnic Institute and State University, 1982.

Loyd D. Andrew is associate professor of higher education at Virginia Polytechnic Institute and State University and senior staff consultant to Science Management Corporation, Washington, D.C.

This case study describes how path analysis and causal modeling were used to assess the impact of federal R&D spending on Ph.D. production at leading research universities. The data base was constructed by integrating five years of data from seven different surveys into a single data base.

Impact Analysis Using an Integrated Data Base: A Case Study

David J. Bowering

This chapter describes how existing data bases can be used to address an evaluation research problem without an extremely expensive and time-consuming original data collection. Although we often will not admit it, there are usually a number of equally valid ways of approaching any given evaluation question, each with its own particular merits and limitations. The choice of one analytical approach over another is often a matter of the researcher's interpretation of the problem, the resources available, and even the researcher's individual taste. Generally, we tend to allow the analysis plan that we choose to drive our definition of data needs.

A point of methodological significance in this study is that the nature of existing data influenced the choice of analytical approach, which in turn influenced the choice of impact measures and the way in which the problem was defined. Although by no means unusual in practice, this is a departure from the conventional approach in which the prob-

The case study described in this chapter is based on work conducted under contract no. SRS–8018112 from the National Science Foundation.

D. J. Bowering (Ed.). *Secondary Analysis of Available Data Bases.* New Directions for Program Evaluation, no. 22. San Francisco: Jossey-Bass, June 1984.

lem definition determines the analysis plans which determines the definition of data requirements, and so on. The conventional practice in evaluation is to define the problem, develop an analysis plan that addresses it, identify and define the data needs, collect the data, and analyze the data. There is nothing wrong with this practice, but it can be limiting, and in the case reported here we chose to depart from it to some extent.

We did not want to perform yet another enumeration study. We wanted instead to measure the effects of possible relationships between federal spending on research and development (R&D) and Ph.D. production, and we wanted to describe those relationships mathematically. Thus, we decided against the usual site visits that gather anecdotal, qualitative expert testimony on the problem of interest. Since funds were limited, we looked first to see what data relevant to the problem were already available in sufficient quantity, quality, and detail. Data from the Higher Education General Information Survey (HEGIS) and the National Science Foundation surveys in science and engineering immediately came to light. Thinking through what was available in these data bases led us to examine analytical approaches to which the data lent themselves that were consistent with the nature of the problem. The process was iterative and led us to clarify our research goals and questions. Eventually, we settled on causal modeling and path analysis as a satisfactory way of assessing how federal spending on academic R&D affects Ph.D. production and other outcomes both directly and also indirectly through intervening variables, such as enrollments (Blalock, 1971; Macdonald and Doreian, 1977). The discussion in this chapter is limited to the effects on Ph.D. production.

The Problem

Traditionally, there has been a close bond between graduate education and research activity in universities and colleges but there is evidence that this relationship is being weakened as the growth of academic research slows (Teich and Lambright, 1981). That this growth is slowing is illustrated by the critical shortages of new graduates in certain areas of science and engineering, particularly the computer sciences and some engineering disciplines, which are felt most acutely at the Ph.D. level. Schools of science and engineering are finding it increasingly difficult to attract new, young faculty (Grodzins, 1980).

At the same time, it is clear that science and engineering research in universities has come to rely heavily on federal support. In fact, recent figures indicate that more than 50 percent of the federally sponsored research in the United States is conducted at universities and colleges, and 85 percent of this research is concentrated in the hundred institutions that lead in R&D expenditures. Thus, it is reasonable to expect that changes in federal sponsorship of academic R&D can have an effect on the graduate programs of institutions that rely heavily on federal research dollars. Studies have attested both to this influence and to the importance of federal investment in academic science and engineering research. However, such studies have generally involved field interviews at universities and colleges rather than statistical analysis of quantitative data, and the few quantitative analyses that have been done are generally enumeration studies. While there has been no shortage of anecdotal testimony about the nature and the importance of the federal influence on research universities, the same cannot be said of studies attempting to quantify these effects.

There are many obstacles to developing quantitative measures of the effects of R&D expenditures on educational outcomes. Not the least of these obstacles lies in the methodological problem of isolating the effects of federally sponsored R&D from the myriad other factors at work, particularly the indirect effects that expenditures have through intervening or concomitant variables. In the past, researchers have typically tried to measure the direct effects above and beyond any indirect effects, and to remove the indirect influences. They have relied on such techniques as stepwise regression analysis. A key feature of the study reported here was the attempt to measure both the direct and the indirect effects.

Another major problem is the attribution of causality. Many studies, particularly enumeration or correlation studies, attribute causality on the basis of correlations between variables without any empirical justification for doing so. Worse, they simply report the association, and the reader is not discouraged from drawing conclusions of causality. Correlation does not establish causation. Even when a correlation is strong, we do not know how much of it is causal and how much of it is the fortuitous result of a joint association with some other factor that is the true causal variable. The path analysis approach that our study took allowed us to separate the potentially causal components of a relationship from the noncausal components. Path analysis does not establish causality, but, given some rational assumptions about causality among the variables, it allows us to separate the effects of causal relationships from the effects of noncausal relationships (Alwin and Hauser, 1975).

Finally, few impact analyses have statistically analyzed the large and growing volume of institutional survey data regularly collected by federal and other agencies. Most impact analyses have undertaken original data-collection efforts, often field surveys involving expensive and time-consuming site visits to institutions. Our study demonstrates that existing institutional data on academic science and engineering collected annually by the National Science Foundation (NSF) can be used to analyze some of the effects of federally sponsored R&D on academic science education and research. The same approach can be applied to a variety of evaluation problems, and we hope that the efforts described here will stimulate others to look to existing data bases for some of their own research efforts.

Study Objectives. The purpose of the study was to assess whether the statistical technique of path analysis could be applied to quantitative survey data on science and engeneering collected by the University and Nonprofit Institutions Studies Group (UNISG) in NSF and by the Higher Education General Information Survey (HEGIS) of the National Center for Education Statistics to yield interpretable, valid, and credible results about the effects of federally sponsored R&D on graduate degree production at leading research universities. Path analysis requires the researcher to formulate, a priori, structural models of the causal linkages between a variable of interest, an outcome, and other intervening variables while controlling for the effects of other factors. The study was restricted to three fields of science, the biological sciences, the physical sciences, and engineering, for no other reason than limitations of resources.

The key to successful application of the path analysis technique is the design of the initial structural model. In this study, the design was developed jointly by the research team and a panel of advisers whose members were selected for their expertise in higher education finance, academic science statistics, science and engineering research, and causal modeling. The design had three objectives: to test the utility of causal modeling and path analysis for assessing the educational effects of federally sponsored R&D in science and engineering at leading research universities, to construct causal models of the direct and indirect effects of these expenditures on Ph.D. production through empirical analysis, and to measure and develop plausible, testable hypotheses about the way in which federally financed R&D in science and engineering affects graduate degree production at universities and colleges.

Research Questions. Five key methodological and substantive questions were formulated in order to address these objectives: First, can path analysis produce a credible causal model? Can the effects of federally sponsored R&D in science and engineering on specified educational outcomes (such as Ph.D. production) be measured using this model? Second, do the models that are developed remain stable over time? Third, do different models emerge for different fields of science? Fourth, do different models emerge for groups of public and private universities? Fifth, what are the effects of federal R&D expenditures in quantitative terms? Are they logical, and does informed opinion consider that they reflect reality?

Scope and Limitations of the Study. It is almost axiomatic that the results of any study reporting on the educational effects of federally sponsored R&D will be the subject of some controversy. Thus, it is important to note the various constraints and limitations on the study and set the project within its proper scope and context.

Establishing causation is a very difficult methodological problem for any study design. It usually implies comparisons with control groups of some kind that enable differences in effects to be detected. However, in causal modeling the term *causation* points to something slightly different: It means an axiomatic sequencing of variables on the basis of logical assumptions about the direction of relationships. Path analysis is a statistical technique for measuring the consequences of the causal sequences for changes in the outcome variables. It does not imply a definitive assessment of the forces that precipitate the causal relationships, nor does it establish causation; rather, it measures the effects of the assumptions about causal relationships between variables. Path analysis does not reveal the root causes of causal relationships, but it can demonstrate their existence, and it can thereby provide focus for subsequent investigations of causality. That is, it provides an a priori mechanism for focusing costly field investigations by pinpointing potentially fruitful areas of inquiry before resources are committed.

The sample used in our study was not probabilistically drawn. Nevertheless, as part of the model-building process, we compared the multiple correlation and regression coefficients with tables of critical values to "test" whether they were statistically greater than zero. We chose to do this as a means of setting criteria for reduction of the initial model.

Conceptual Framework

The fundamental proposition underlying our study was that there is a functional relationship between federal R&D expenditures at academic institutions and certain institutional outcomes, such as grad-

quantitatively analyze causal relationships among them. Path analysis is a statistical technique for quantitatively analyzing the direct and indirect effects of a variable of interest (such as federally sponsored R&D) on an outcome variable (such as Ph.D. production) with which it is hypothesized to have a linear causal relationship (Wolfle, 1980).

Given some assumptions or evidence about the causal relationships among variables, path analysis permits the researcher to break down the relationships into causal and noncausal components and to measure the direct and indirect effects of the variable of interest while holding other variables constant. For example, institutional variables can be included in the model as exogenous or control variables, and their effects on the outcomes can thereby by controlled. Our study calculated two types of impacts attributable to federally sponsored R&D expenditures: the number of standard deviations change in Ph.D. production that was attributed to one standard deviation change in federal R&D expenditures, other variables in the model being held constant, and the actual change in Ph.D. production that was attributed to $1 million in federal R&D expenditures, other variables in the model being held constant.

Path Analysis and Causal Modeling. The concepts of causal modeling and path analysis can best be conveyed through illustration. However, the causal sequencing in the illustrations in this section is not intended to represent definitive relationships among the variables. Identifying the appropriate causal sequencing is part of the model-building process and involves input from a variety of information sources.

Suppose that we wish to examine the way in which federal R&D support to university programs influences a particular educational outcome, such as graduate student enrollment. We can hypothesize a direct influence due to assistantships or direct support that allows students who would not otherwise be able to pursue graduate study for financial reason to do so. Figure 1 illustrates this hypothesis.

However R&D dollars may exert other, less direct influences.

Figure 1.

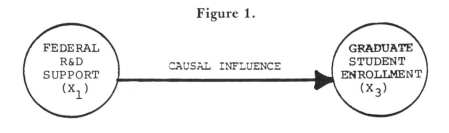

For example, we can hypothesize that an increase (or decrease) in R&D dollars influences faculty hiring, presumably in a direct, not an inverse, way. This increase (or decrease) in professional staff size in turn influences the size of the graduate student enrollment that the department can accommodate. If such a relationship exists, then it can be said that federal R&D spending (X_1) has an indirect influence on graduate student enrollment (X_4) through its effects on professional staff size (X_2). This situation is illustrated in Figure 2.

We now have hypothesized two paths of influence, the direct path, X_1X_4, and the indirect path, $X_1X_2X_4$. At this point, we can hypothesize further that federal R&D support (X_1) influences institutional policy regarding the commitment of institutional resources, such as the dedication of physical plant or real estate. This in turn may require the institution to increase its allocations of operating funds (X_3), and increased facilities and operating funds in turn may influence graduate student enrollment (X_4) by both attracting students and accommodating them. Figure 3 illustrates this hypothesis.

Other factors may then enter the picture. State appropriations, nongovernmental R&D support, and the national economy are just some of the variables that can enter the increasingly complex structural model. In this way, a hypothetical model can be constructed of the various paths by which a variable of interest, such as federal R&D expenditures, affects the outcomes of interest. In Figure 3, the outcome variable is graduate student enrollment, but any outcome can be used, provided it can be quantified in some way and axiomatic causal relationships with other independent, causal variables can be postulated. The next step

Figure 2.

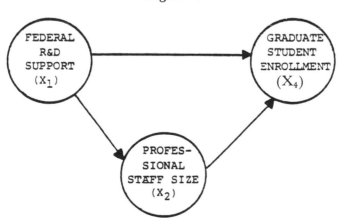

Figure 3.

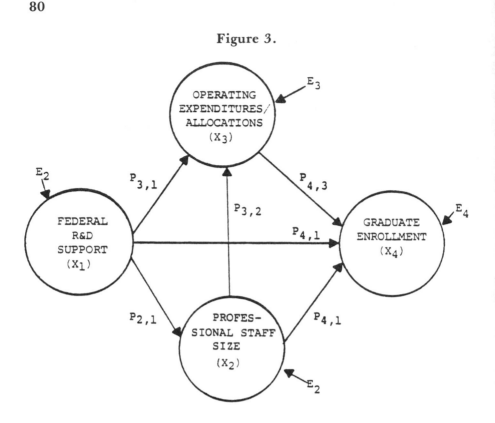

in the process is to measure the strength of the specified causal relationships between the variables and the causal sequences. By the strength of a relationship between two variables in a causal chain, we mean the amount of change in one variable that results from a unit change in a preceding variable, with the other variables being held constant. This change is called a path coefficient. In Figure 3, the path coefficients are denoted by P_{ij}.

Two types of path coefficients can be used, depending on the researcher's purposes. The unstandardized coefficient is expressed in the natural units of the variables. The standardized path coefficient is the number of standard deviations change in one variable that results from a one standard deviation change in an antecedent variable, with other variables being held constant. Our study used both types of path coefficients. To illustrate, suppose that Figure 3 represents a plausible model of the manner in which outcome variable X_4 (graduate student enrollment) is influenced by causal variable X_1 (federal R&D spending), and reduce it to Figure 4: The various Es represent exogenous variables—influences outside the model. Direct effect of X_1 on X_4 is

Figure 4.

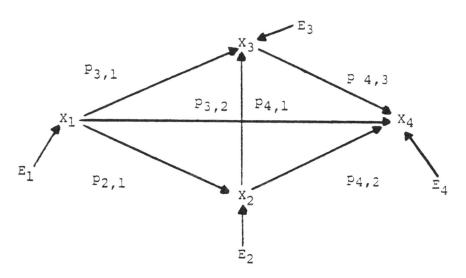

represented by the path coefficient $P_{4,1}$. There are also three indirect paths: $X_1 \rightarrow X_3 \rightarrow X_4$, $X_1 \rightarrow X_2 \rightarrow X_4$, and $X_1 \rightarrow X_2 \rightarrow X_3 \rightarrow X_4$. Three structural equations describe the model:

$$X_4 = P_{4,1}(X_1) + P_{4,2}(X_2) + P_{4,3}(X_3) + E_4$$
$$X_3 = P_{3,1}(X_1) + P_{3,2}(X_2) + E_3$$
$$X_2 = P_{2,1}(X_1) + E_2$$

Multiple regressions for each of these linear equations will generate regression weights, which are in fact the path coefficients P_{ij} (Duncan, 1975).

The next step is to calculate the direct and indirect effects of X_1 on X_4. Indirect effects are calculated by the products of the path coefficients. The direct effect is $P_{4,1}$. The three indirect effects are:

$$X_1 \rightarrow X_3 \rightarrow X_4 = (P_{3,1})(P_{4,3})$$
$$X_1 \rightarrow X_2 \rightarrow X_4 = (P_{2,1})(P_{4,2})$$
$$X_1 \rightarrow X_2 \rightarrow X_3 = (P_{2,1})(P_{3,2})(P_{4,3})$$

The total linear causal effect coefficient $C_{4,1}$ is:

(1) $C_{4,1} = P_{4,1} + [(P_{3,1})(P_{4,3})] + [(P_{2,1})(P_{4,2})] + [(P_{2,1})(P_{3,2})(P_{4,3})]$

Substitution of the standardized coefficients in equation 1 will give a measure of the number of standard deviations change in graduate degree production (X_4) that can be attributed to a one standard deviation change in federal R&D expenditures (X_1), with the other variables being held constant. Effects can be measured in the natural units of the variables, but if the objective is to compare effects, then comparisons can only be made if the coefficients refer to the same scales (Macdonald, 1977). In such a case standardized coefficients are preferable to unstandardized coefficients.

The Structural Model. The initial structural model used as the starting point for our path analysis is presented in schematic form in Figure 5. Variables X_4 and X_6 are missing from the structural model. The panel recommended including two variables that proved impractical, and they were dropped early in the analysis. Clearly, the model is rather complex and cumbersome, but the path analysis simplified it considerably, as we expected. The set of structural equations that describes the model is presented here. The path coefficients (P_{ij}) in the equations are the regression weights produced through regression analysis. Regression analyses were run for each equation to determine the path coefficients and to develop the causal models described in a later section. The variables shown in Figure 5 are defined in the following section.

$$X_{15} = P_{15,1}(X_1) + P_{15,3}(X_3) + P_{15,5}(X_5) + P_{15,7}(X_7)$$
$$+ P_{15,8}(X_8) + P_{15,9}(X_9) + P_{15,10}(X_{10}) + P_{15,11}(X_{11}) + P_{15,12}(X_{12})$$
$$+ P_{15,13}(X_{13}) + P_{15,14}(X_{14}) + E_{14}$$

$$X_{14} = P_{14,1}(X_1) + P_{14,2}(X_2) + P_{14,3}(X_3) + P_{14,5}(X_5) + P_{14,7}(X_7)$$
$$+ P_{14,8}(X_8) + P_{14,9}(X_9) + P_{14,10}(X_{10}) + P_{14,11}(X_{11}) + P_{14,12}(X_{12})$$
$$+ P_{14,13}(X_{13}) + P_{14,14}(X_{14}) + E_{14}$$

$$X_{13} = P_{13,1}(X_1) + P_{13,2}(X_2) + P_{13,3}(X_3) + P_{13,5}(X_5) + P_{13,7}(X_7)$$
$$+ P_{13,8}(X_8) + P_{13,9}(X_9) + P_{13,10}(X_{10}) + P_{13,11}(X_{11}) + P_{13,12}(X_{12})$$
$$+ P_{13,13}(X_{13}) + P_{13,14}(X_{14}) + E_{13}$$

$$X_{12} = P_{12,1}(X_1) + P_{12,2}(X_2) + P_{12,3}(X_3) + P_{12,5}(X_5) + P_{12,7}(X_7)$$
$$+ P_{12,8}(X_8) + P_{12,9}(X_9) + P_{12,10}(X_{10}) + P_{12,11}(X_{11}) + P_{12,12}(X_{12})$$
$$+ P_{12,13}(X_{13}) + P_{12,14}(X_{14}) + E_{11}$$

Each of these equations was the subject of regression analysis with the SPSS package to determine the values of the path coefficients (P_{ij}). Effect coefficients were calculated from the path coefficients, and the direct, indirect, and total causal effects of federal R&D expenditures on the outcomes were analyzed and quantified. The discussion in this chapter is limited to the effects on Ph.D. production (X_{15}).

Figure 5. Structural Model Used in the Path Analyses

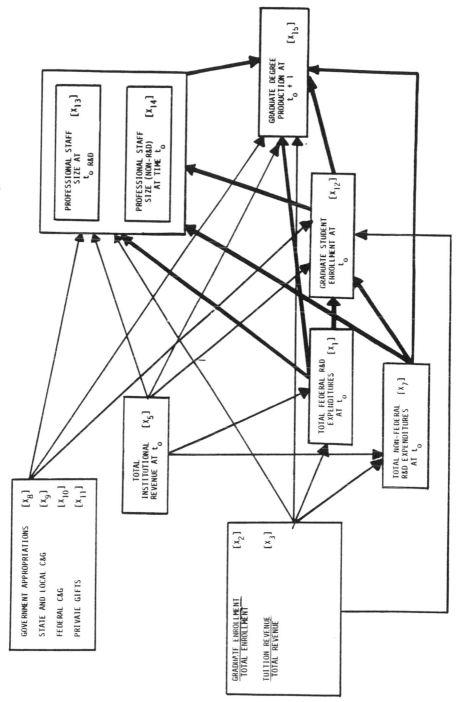

Methodology

There were seven steps in our study. First, we identified and defined the independent, intervening, and outcome variables to be used in the structural model. Second, we postulated an initial structural model of the ways in which federal R&D expenditures and other variables interact to affect the outcomes. That is, we specified plausible causal sequences among the variables, including lag and lead relationships, as the basis for statistical analysis. Third, from the HEGIS and UNISG data tapes, we developed an integrated data base containing data on the variables specified in the model. Fourth, we applied path analysis techniques to the empirical data in order to measure the strength of the relationships specified in the model and compute path coefficients. We removed the paths whose coefficients were not statistically greater than zero, constructed a reduced model, and ran the regressions again in order to determine new coefficients. Next, we tested the reduced model to determine whether removing the paths had caused it to deteriorate, and we made any necessary adjustments. Then, we performed additional runs until all the path coefficients in the model were nonzero. Fifth, we quantified the direct and indirect effects of federal R&D expenditures by computing effect coefficients. Sixth, we asked experts in academic science to compare the empirically derived models and results with reality. Seventh, we developed testable quantitative and qualitative hypotheses about the effects and drew conclusions about the utility of path analysis as a way of analyzing the direct and indirect effects of federal R&D dollars on Ph.D. production in universities and other institutions of higher education. This section examines these seven steps.

Step One: Identify Variables to Be Included in the Data Base. Development of appropriate independent and intervening variables to include in the model is key to the entire process. In our study, development was accomplished through discussion with researchers in academic science statistics, institutional researchers in higher education, and practitioners at universities who had the requisite experience, knowledge, and insight about the interactive processes at their institutions. The principal mechanism was an evaluation panel workshop. One of its main activities was a critique of the list of variables. During the evaluation panel review, problems posed for these variables by the existing data bases were discussed. Potential threats to the validity of the results were identified, and methods for reducing validity problems were sought both in round table working sessions and from individual panel members.

Step Two. Specify Causal Sequences and Construct Plausible Structural Models. Step two represented our first effort at constructing a priori causal models. The development of these models took place through several activities. The literature was one source of information about appropriate causal relationships. The insight and experience of evaluation panel members was another. In fact, the most critical product of the panel members' effort was their input to the models used to perform the path analyses. Our goal in the initial modeling effort was to produce a single inclusive model that could be used with path analysis to derive a reduced model or models. Our a priori model is presented schematically in Figure 5.

Step Three: Data Base Development and Verification. Our data base consisted of five years of survey data (1975–1979) for seventy-three of the hundred institutions that led in science and engineering R&D expenditures. The survey data were collected by the Universities and Nonprofit Institutions Studies Group (UNISG) of the National Science Foundation (NSF) and the National Center for Education Statistics (NCES) in seven annual surveys: the NSF survey of scientific and engineering expenditures at universities and colleges, the joint NSF and National Institutes of Health survey of graduate science students and postdoctorates, the NSF survey of scientists and engineers employed at universities and colleges, the NCES survey of salaries, tenure, and fringe benefits of full-time instructional faculty, the NCES survey of financial statistics of institutions of higher education, the NCES survey of degrees and other formal awards conferred, and the NCES survey of fall enrollment in institutions of higher education.

Data from these surveys were integrated on a single tape structured to facilitate our analyses. Software was developed to select specified data elements from each of the seven surveys, and detailed documentation specifying such things as layout, data elements, field lengths, and descriptors was developed for the integrated data tape. Table 1 describes the variables included in each record and identifies the surveys from which they were drawn. Table 2 lists the seventy-three institutions included in the data base.

The integrated data tape was tailored to meet the particular needs of this study, and its record structure was relatively complex. For this reasons, data verification efforts consisted of two phases. First, the data on the integrated tape were compared with institutional profiles supplied by the NSF to ensure that they correctly reflected the survey data reported by the institution. Second, the data on the tape were compared with actual university records for a sample of institutions.

Table 1. Variables Included in the Structural Model

VARIABLE	VARIABLE DESCRIPTION	COMMENTS	YEARS	DATA SOURCE
X_1	FEDERAL R&D EXPENDITURES IN S&E . ENGINEERING . BIOLOGICAL SCIENCES . PHYSICAL SCIENCES	-----	FISCAL 1975-1979	SURVEY OF SCIENTIFIC AND ENGINEERING EXPENDITURES AT UNIVERSITIES AND COLLEGES, NATIONAL SCIENCE FOUNDATION
X_2	PROPORTION OF INSTITUTIONAL REVENUE WHICH IS TUITION REVENUE	CONTROL FOR EFFECT OF INSTITUTIONAL SIZE ON DEGREE PRODUCTION AND FACULTY GROWTH/DECLINE	FISCAL 1975-1979	FINANCIAL STATISTICS OF INSTITUTIONS OF HIGHER EDUCATION, HIGHER EDUCATION GENERAL INFORMATION SURVEYS, NCES
X_3	PROPORTION OF INSTITUTIONAL ENROLLMENT WHICH IS GRADUATE ENROLLMENT	CONTROL FOR EFFECT OF INSTITUTIONAL SIZE ON DEPARTMENTAL ENROLLMENTS (GRADUATE)	FALL 1975-1979	FALL ENROLLMENT AND COMPLIANCE REPORT OF INSTITUTIONS OF HIGHER EDUCATION, HIGHER EDUCATION GENERAL INFORMATION SURVEYS, NCES
X_5	TOTAL INSTITUTIONAL REVENUES	CONTROL FOR INCREASE IN SIZE OF INSTITUTIONAL RESOURCES	FISCAL 1975-1979	FINANCIAL STATISTICS OF INSTITUTIONS OF HIGHER EDUCATION, HIGHER EDUCATION GENERAL INFORMATION SURVEYS, NCES
X_7	NON FEDERAL R&D EXPENDITURES . ENGINEERING . BIOLOGICAL SCIENCES . PHYSICAL SCIENCES	-----	FISCAL 1975-1979	SURVEY OF SCIENTIFIC AND ENGINEERING EXPENDITURES AT UNIVERSITIES AND COLLEGES, NATIONAL SCIENCE FOUNDATION
X_8, X_9, X_{10}, X_{11}	INSTITUTIONAL REVENUES FROM DIFFERENT SOURCES AT TIME t_0 . GOVERNMENT APPROPRIATIONS (X_8) . STATE AND LOCAL CONTRACTS AND GRANTS (X_9) . FEDERAL CONTRACTS AND GRANTS (X_{10}) . PRIVATE GIFTS (X_{11})	-----	FISCAL 1975-1979	FINANCIAL STATISTICS OF INSTITUTIONS OF HIGHER EDUCATION, HIGHER EDUCATION GENERAL INFORMATION SURVEYS, NCES

VARIABLE	VARIABLE DESCRIPTION	COMMENTS	YEARS	DATA SOURCE
X_{12}	ENROLLMENTS (MA + PH.D.) . ENGINEERING . BIOLOGICAL SCIENCES . PHYSICAL SCIENCES	TOTAL HEADCOUNT CANNOT SEPARATE MAs AND PH.Ds TOTALS ARE OBTAINED FROM NSF STUDENT SUPPORT SURVEY FIRST-YEAR, FULL-TIME HEADCOUNT	FALL 1975-1979 1975-1979	SURVEY OF GRADUATE SCIENCE STUDENT SUPPORT AND POSTDOCTORALS, NATIONAL SCIENCE FOUNDATION/NATIONAL INSTITUTES OF HEALTH
X_{13}	SIZE OF THE R&D STAFF . ENGINEERING . BIOLOGICAL SCIENCES . PHYSICAL SCIENCES	HEADCOUNT OF PROFESSIONAL STAFF WHO ARE PRIMARILY INVOLVED IN R&D RATHER THAN INSTRUCTION AS DEFINED BY NSF (CUT-OFF NOT SPECIFIED) FTES OF R&D PROFESSIONAL STAFF	JANUARY 1975-1978 JANUARY 1978-1979	SURVEY OF SCIENTIFIC AND ENGINEERING PERSONNEL EMPLOYED AT UNIVERSITIES AND COLLEGES, NATIONAL SCIENCE FOUNDATION
X_{14}	SIZE OF THE INSTRUCTIONAL STAFF . ENGINEERING . BIOLOGICAL SCIENCES . PHYSICAL SCIENCES	HEADCOUNT OF PROFESSIONAL STAFF WHO ARE PRIMARILY INVOLVED IN TEACHING, AS DEFINED BY NSF (CUT-OFF NOT SPECIFIED) FTES OF NON-R&D STAFF TOTAL FTES IN S&E ARE AVAILABLE	JANUARY 1975-1978 1978-1979 1975-1979	SURVEY OF SCIENTIFIC AND ENGINEERING PERSONNEL EMPLOYED AT UNIVERSITIES AND COLLEGES, NATIONAL SCIENCE FOUNDATION
X_{15}	GRADUATE DEGREE PRODUCTION . ENGINEERING . BIOLOGICAL SCIENCES . PHYSICAL SCIENCES	ANALYSIS WAS DONE BY EACH CLASS OF DEGREE SEPARATELY	ACADEMIC YEAR 1975-1979	DEGREES AND OTHER FORMAL AWARDS CONFERRED, HIGHER EDUCATION GENERAL INFORMATION SURVEYS, NCES

Table 2. Universities in the Data Base (N = 73)

PUBLIC

- UNIVERSITY OF WISCONSIN - MADISON
- UNIVERSITY OF CALIFORNIA - SAN DIEGO
- UNIVERSITY OF WASHINGTON
- UNIVERSITY OF ILLINOIS - URBANA
- UNIVERSITY OF CALIFORNIA - LOS ANGELES

- UNIVERSITY OF CALIFORNIA - BERKELEY
- UNIVERSITY OF TEXAS AT AUSTIN
- UNIVERSITY OF CALIFORNIA - SAN FRANCISCO
- MICHIGAN STATE UNIVERSITY
- UNIVERSITY OF CALIFORNIA - DAVIS

- UNIVERSITY OF FLORIDA
- UNIVERSITY OF GEORGIA
- UNIVERSITY OF ARIZONA
- IOWA STATE UNIVE-SITY OF SCIENCE AND TECHNOLOGY
- COLORADO STATE UNIVERSITY

- OREGON STATE UNIVERSITY
- UNIVERSITY OF UTAH
- NORTH CAROLINA STATE UNIVERSITY AT RALEIGH
- UNIVERSITY OF MARYLAND - COLLEGE PARK
- UNIVERSITY OF HAWAII - MANOA

- UNIVERSITY OF MISSOURI - COLUMBIA
- UNIVERSITY OF NORTH CAROLINA AT CHAPEL HILL
- UNIVERSITY OF IOWA
- VIRGINIA POLYTECHNIC INSTITUTE & STATE UNIVERSITY
- UNIVERSITY OF NEBRASKA - LINCOLN

- UNIVERSITY OF ALABAMA - BIRMINGHAM
- WASHINGTON STATE UNIVERSITY
- WAYNE STATE UNIVERSITY
- UNIVERSITY OF TEXAS HEALTH SCIENCE CENTER - DALLAS
- FLORIDA STATE UNIVERSITY

- UNIVERSITY OF MASSACHUSETTS - AMHERST
- UNIVERSITY OF CALIFORNIA - IRVINE
- UTAH STATE UNIVERSITY
- UNIVERSITY OF VERMONT & STATE AGRICULTURAL COLLEGE
- INDIANA UNIVERSITY - PURDUE UNIVERSITY - INDIANAPOLIS

- INDIANA UNIVERSITY - BLOOMINGTON
- VIRGINIA COMMONWEALTH UNIVERSITY
- UNIVERSITY OF RHODE ISLAND
- UNIVERSITY OF MARYLAND - MALTIOMRE PROF. SCHOOL
- UNIVERSITY OF TENNESSEE - KNOXVILLE

- UNIVERSITY OF ILLINOIS MEDICAL CENTER
- UNIVERSITY OF OREGON HEALTH SCIENCE CENTER
- SUNY DOWNSTATE MEDICAL CENTER
- UNIVERSITY OF CALIFORNIA SANTA BARBARA

PRIVATE

- MASSACHUSETTS INSTITUTE OF TECHNOLOGY
- STANFORD UNIVERSITY
- HARVARD UNIVERSITY
- UNIVERSITY OF PENNSYLVANIA
- COLUMBIA UNIVERSITY - MAIN DIVISION

- JOHNS HOPKINS UNIVERSITY
- UNIVERSITY OF CHICAGO
- NEW YORK UNIVERSITY
- UNIVERSITY OF ROCHESTER
- YALE UNIVERSITY

- UNIVERSITY OF SOUTHERN CALIFORNIA
- WASHINGTON UNIVERSITY
- UNIVERSITY OF MIAMI
- ROCKFELLER UNIVERSITY
- DUKE UNIVERSITY

- YESHIVA UNIVERSITY
- NORTHWESTERN UNIVERSITY
- CASE WESTERN RESERVE UNIVERSITY
- CALIFORNIA INSTITUTE OF TECHNOLOGY
- CARNEGIE-MELLON UNIVERSITY

- PRINCETON UNIVERSITY
- GEORGE WASHINGTON UNIVERSITY
- BOSTON UNIVERSITY
- VANDERBILT UNIVERSITY
- EMORY UNIVERSITY

- BROWN UNIVERSITY
- UNIVERSITY OF DAYTON
- GEORGETOWN UNIVERSITY
- UNIVERSITY OF DENVER

Examination of Trend Data. A sample of data elements was selected for each of the seven surveys, and trend data for the 1975–1979 period were inspected for all seventy-three institutions. An eyeball examination was made to flag any dramatic departures from expected values. Where such departures were observed, a detailed examination of all the data was made, which sometimes entailed checking at the source. For example, knowledge of one institution suggested that enrollments in the physical sciences were surprisingly high. Further investigation revealed that the data were from agriculture, which was consistent with the nature of the institution. This points up the need for those performing verification activities to have some knowledge of the sample. Trends in the data were also compared with data published in the National Science Foundation's academic science reports and statistical tables and with the National Center for Education Statistics's *Digest of Education Statistics* (1975–1979).

Verification of Data at a Sample of Universities. The second phase of the verification plan involved comparison of the data for all variables with institutional records of twelve universities. A university profile on all variables was developed and forwarded to each institution for verification against university records. The profiles consisted of nine tables and verification involved the use of imputed values for the same data the integrated data base. Each university was asked to make any necessary changes on the profile itself and to advise us of any significant management, administrative, or financial changes during the five-year period (for example, opening or closing a branch or drastic changes in accounting or reporting procedures) that might affect the data. Eight of the twelve institutions replied.

Results of Data-Verification Activities. The data-verification activities did not result in substantive changes to the data base. With only a few minor exceptions, university respondents confirmed that the profiles accurately reflected the data for their institutions.

Twenty-seven of the hundred R&D institutions were excluded from the data base, because inconsistencies in FICE codes from survey to survey and from year to year made it impossible to develop complete records for them. In addition, branches and medical schools were treated differently within the FICE code structure by different institutions.

One area of concern that arose during data base development and verification involved the use of imputed valued for the same data field over several years. In several cases, institutions reported that the data were believed to be incorrect, but they had no records from which to determine the proper data values.

Aggregation of data was found to be necessary in order to reflect the same measure across institutions. For example, full-time instructional faculty is reported in HEGIS in two categories: faculty on nine- or ten-month contracts and faculty on eleven- or twelve-month contracts. These data were aggregated in our data file, since they reflect differences in management and administrative practices rather than different measures.

Step Four: Apply Path Analysis to Construct Reduced Models. Step four involved the first statistical analysis of the data base. In step four, we used multiple regression analysis to compute path coefficients and path effects for the structural model. The goal was to produce a reduced model that best fit the data.

The analysis plan called for elimination of trivial linkages, development of sets of equations that described the reduced models, and use of structural equations to develop effect measures. This plan was accomplished in the following way: Multiple regressions were run with the initial model to determine the standardized and unstandardized regression weights, which were the path coefficients in the model, and to assess the model's completeness. The paths for which the coefficients were not statistically different from zero were removed from the model. Next, the regression was rerun to determine the coefficients of the reduced model. The reduced model was tested to see whether there had been a deterioration from the original model. The model was adjusted as necessary, and the final regression runs were made to determine the set of nonzero path coefficients that described the model. Finally these procedures were repeated for subsamples of public and private universities for each of the three areas of science.

Assessing the Completeness of the Model. The square of the multiple correlation coefficient was used as a measure of the strength of the regression relationships. The multiple correlation coefficient R for each regression analysis was tested for statistical significance at the .05 level using the F statistic. We recognize that tests of statistical significance are usually applied to probabilistic samples from which generalizations are made to a larger population. However, we chose to use such tests as benchmark criteria for developing parsimonious models.

The square of R was used to measure the goodness of fit between the data and the structural model. This fit was an indicator of whether the models were well specified by the variables. R^2 is a measure of the amount of variance in the outcome that was accounted for by variations in the antecedent variables, expressed as a percent. Values of 70 percent and above were considered to be indicators of strong linear regression relationships between the outcomes and the antecedent variables.

Reduction of the Initial Model. The path coefficients produced in the regression analysis, which was performed with the SPSS package, were accompanied in the output by t statistics. These t statistics were used to test the statistical significance of the path coefficients, which were compared against critical values of t at the .05 level of statistical significance. Coefficients that exceeded the critical values were considered to be nonzero coefficients, and they were retained in the reduced model, while coefficients that did not exceed the critical values were removed.

The regressions were then run again to produce new path coefficients for the reduced model.

There is an important consideration when paths are removed from the model in this way. When a single path is deleted, the situation is simple, and the t statistic is tested at the appropriate level of significance and degrees of freedom. When more than one path is deleted, the usual t test for one coefficient cannot be used. Instead, an F test that measures the deterioration in the goodness of fit between the full model and the reduced model must be used. We computed the following F statistic (Macdonald, 1977):

$$F = \frac{(RSS_R - RSS_U)/k}{(RS_U/n - p - 1)}$$

where RSS_R is the residual sum of squares of the reduced model, RSS_U is the residual sum of squares of the unreduced model, k is the number of variables removed, n is the number of universities in the sample, and p is the number of variables in the unreduced model. This statistic was compared with the critical values at k and $n - p - 1$ degrees of freedom. If the computed F was greater than the critical value, then the reduced model was significantly different from the initial one; variables were replaced, and the procedure was repeated until no significant deterioration occurred. In this way, after two reductions, structural models were developed that could be used to analyze effects. Sets of path coefficients were identified, sets of structural equations were constructed, and effects were calculated.

Step Five: Compare Empirically Derived Models with Reality and Reanalyze the Data. The purpose of step five was to obtain the views of panel members and others on the extent to which the reduced and reconstructed models matched their experience of the reality of their institutions. Statements about the strengths of the statistical linkages and the causal sequences among the variables were presented for the panel's reaction at a second evaluation panel workshop.

Step Six: Quantify Direct and Indirect Effects. In step six, the full statistical path analysis of the models was performed to analyze the magnitude of direct and indirect effects of variables on the outcome. A complete path analysis was made to decompose the simple association between R&D funding and the outcome variables into the direct and indirect effects. Structural equations that described the models were constructed, and hypotheses regarding the relationships among the variables were developed from these equations.

Step Seven: Develop Quantitative and Qualitative Hypotheses and Assess the Utility of the Analytical Approach. The outcome of the first six steps was a set of models with specifications that included structural schematics graphically displaying the interrelationships among variables and the direction of linkages among variables (inverse or direct), structural equations describing the mathematical relationships among variables and between independent variables and Ph.D. production, and measures of the total effect and of the direct and the indirect effects of R&D funding on Ph.D. production.

Four analyses were conducted to build the models and assess the causal effects. First, path analysis was applied to each year of data for the group of seventy-three universities in the 1975–1979 period for each of the three fields of science—engineering, physical sciences, and biological sciences. A model was constructed for each field of science, and the stability of the models over time was assessed in terms of the variability in path coefficients and the variables in the models.

Second, the total sample of seventy-three universities was divided into two groups of forty-four public institutions and twenty-nine private institutions. Analyses identical to those conducted with the total sample were performed for each year of data for the two groups, and models were constructed for both groups for each year in each of the three fields of science. This enabled us to compare and contrast the effects on public and private institutions.

Third, in keeping with panel recommendations and the limited number of years of data, only one analysis with lagged variables was performed. The outcome variable, Ph.D. production, was lagged three years behind the other variables. That is, Ph.D. data for 1978 were regressed against data on the antecedent variables for 1975. The results differed very little from the results of analyses with current data on all variables.

Fourth, two measures of effect were constructed from the standardized and unstandardized path coefficients: The standardized effect of federal R&D expenditures was defined as the number of standard deviations change in an outcome variable that can be attributed to one standard deviation change in federal R&D expenditures, with other variables being held constant. The unstandardized effect of federal R&D expenditures was defined as the actual change in an outcome variable that can be attributed to $1 million in federal R&D expenditures, with other variables being held constant. In the next two sections, the results of these analyses are presented. The first discusses the causal models, and the second discusses the measured effects.

The structural models and equations presented in this section were used to calculate the effects discussed in the next section. We constructed three models: one for the physical sciences, one for the biological sciences, and one for engineering. We also constructed models for private and public universities, but they are not discussed here.

The Physical Sciences Model. The structural model for the physical sciences is presented in Figure 6. The paths in the model are those which remained after two reductions. Figure 6 describes a causal model common to all years of data. There were only minor variations from year to year in the strengths of the linkages between variables.

Several features of the model stand out: First, federal R&D expenditures (X_1) had a direct impact on Ph.D. production, but nonfederal R&D expenditures did not; they affected only R&D staff size (X_{13}). Second, there are no causal linkages between Ph.D. degree production (X_{15}) and size of the professional staff primarily employed in R&D (X_{13}) or persons primarily employed in teaching (X_{14}). In this, the physical sciences model differed from the models for other disciplines. Third, the singly indirect effect of federal R&D expenditures (X_1) on Ph.D. production (X_{15}) was through its effects on graduate student enrollment (X_{12}), as might be expected. Fourth, of the controls for institutional size $(X_2, X_3,$ and $X_5)$, only total institutional revenue (X_5) had a significant effect on Ph.D. production (X_{15}). This was true for all three fields of science. Fifth and most important, the order of magnitude of the path coefficients was constant from year to year; no sudden shifts were observed. This is an important piece of evidence that the causal model describes relationships in the data that were stable over time.

The role of federal R&D dollars in the model is highlighted by the observation that nonfederal R&D expenditures made almost no impact at all. This may be due partly to the lower level of expenditures, since federal R&D expenditures were approximately four times the nonfederal expenditures each year for the universities that we studied.

The general structural equations that describe the reduced models are:

$$X_{15} = P_{15,1}(X_1) + P_{15,5}(X_5) + P_{15,12}(X_{12}) + E_{15}$$

$$X_{12} = P_{12,1}(X_1) + P_{12,5}(X_5) + P_{12,8}(X_8) + E_{12}$$

where P_{ij} are the standardized path coefficients of variable X_j on X_i, and E_i, is the effect unaccounted for by the model equal to $1 - R^2$, where R is the multiple correlation coefficient.

The path coefficients, P_{ij}, are presented in Appendix A for all

Figure 6. Structural Model of the Effects of Federal R&D Expenditures on Graduate Degree Production, for the Years 1975–1979 for the Physical Sciences ($N = 73$)

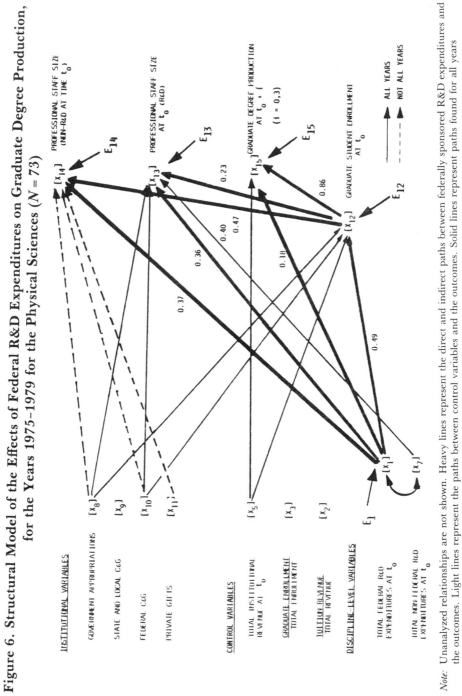

Note: Unanalyzed relationships are not shown. Heavy lines represent the direct and indirect paths between federally sponsored R&D expenditures and the outcomes. Light lines represent the paths between control variables and the outcomes. Solid lines represent paths found for all years of data. Broken lines represent paths found only for some years of data.

three fields of science. The structural equations for a particular year are established by substituting the appropriate coefficents in the general equations above. For example, the equations for 1978 are:

$$X_{15} = 0.18(X_1) - 0.27(X_5) + 0.86(X_{12}) + 0.08$$
$$X_{12} = 0.49(X_1) + 0.23(X_5) + 0.42(X_8) + 0.24$$

The Biological Sciences Model. Development of the biological sciences model followed roughly the same procedures as those described for the physical sciences model. The resulting model is presented in Figure 7. The path coefficients for the biological sciences model were considerably less stable over the five sets of data than they were for the physical sciences or engineering.

The structural equations that describe the reduced model are:

$$X_{15} = P_{15,1}(X_1) + P_{15,5}(X_5) + P_{15,12}(X_{12}) + P_{15,13}(X_{13}) + E_{15}$$
$$X_{13} = P_{13,1}(X_1) + P_{13,5}(X_5) + P_{13,7}(X_7) + P_{13,9}(X_9)$$
$$P_{13,10}(X_{10}) + P_{13,11}(X_{11}) + P_{13,12}(X_{12}) + E_{13}$$
$$X_{12} = P_{12,1}(X_1) + P_{12,8}(X_8) + E_{12}$$

Because of the instability of some of the path coefficients from year to year, no single set of structural equations described a single causal model linking expenditures to Ph.D. production. However, the model constructed for a specific year did fit the data for that year quite well, as indicated by the percents of explained variance (R^2), but not nearly as well as it did for the data on engineering and physical sciences.

The results obtained with the data on biological sciences differed so consistently from the results on physical sciences and engineering that we consider it useful to point out the differences and similarities. First, the only consistent linkage between federal R&D expenditures and Ph.D. production was through its indirect effect on graduate enrollments $(X_1 \rightarrow X_{12} \rightarrow X_{15})$. In this, the biological sciences model differed from the engineering and physical sciences models, in which there was a direct link between the two variables $(X_1 \rightarrow X_{15})$. Second, there was no linkage between size of teaching staff and Ph.D. production in physical sciences. Third, institutional size, as measured by total institutional revenues (X_5), emerged as a control on degree production, just as it did in the physical sciences. Fourth, institutional variables generally played a greater role in the biological sciences model than they did in either the physical sciences or engineering models. Fifth, as in the physical sciences model, nonfederal R&D expenditures showed a relationship only with size of professional R&D staff.

Figure 7. Structural Model of the Effects of Federal R&D Expenditures on Graduate Degree Production, for the Years 1975–1979 for the Biological Sciences (N = 73)

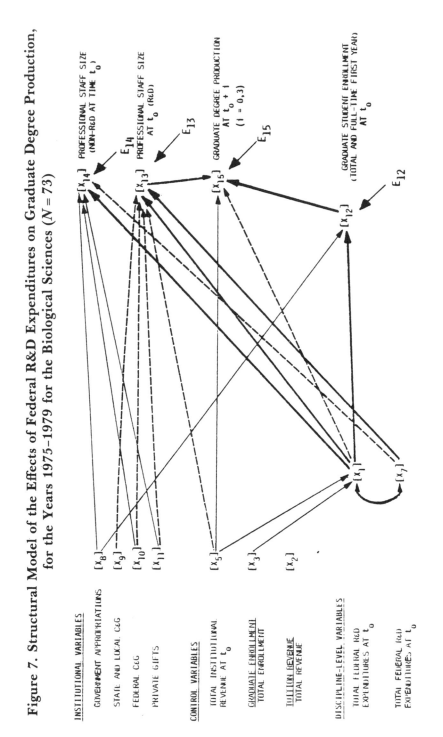

Note: Solid lines represent paths found for all years of data. Broken lines represent paths found only for some years of data.

The Engineering Model. The structural model for engineering is depicted in Figure 8. This model is quite similar to the model for the physical sciences both for the causal paths that emerged and for the stability of the model over several years of data. With the exception of the link between graduate degree production and size of R&D staff, the paths shown in the model were consistent across all years.

Ph.D. production was affected by federal R&D expenditures (X_1), but it was not associated with nonfederal R&D expenditures (X_7). As in the physical sciences, nonfederal expenditures had an effect only on size of professional staff. Institutional size, as measured by total institutional revenues, did not appear to moderate effects on Ph.D. production in any significant way, as it did in the biological and physical sciences.

The structural equations that describe the model are:

$$X_{15} = P_{15,1}(X_1) + P_{15,12}(X_{12}) + P_{15,13}(X_{13}) + E_{15}$$

$$X_{13} = P_{13,1}(X_1) + P_{13,8}(X_8) + P_{13,10}(X_{10}) + P_{13,11}(X_{11}) + P_{13,12}(X_{12}) + E_{13}$$

$$X_{12} = P_{12,1}(X_1) + P_{12,8}(X_8) + E_{12}$$

The linkages among variables in the structural equations for engineering were stronger than they were for the physical and biological sciences. The direct effects of federal R&D expenditures were similar to those for the physical sciences but larger, and the structural model for engineering was generally more firmly established than the models for the other two fields of science.

The structural model fitted the data very well. The multiple correlations, R, were all large and statistically significant, and the percentages of explained variance in the outcomes, R^2, were high, reaching 97 percent in one instance. The values of R^2 are presented in the Tables A1, A2, A3 in Appendix A. Not only were they high, but they were also very close in magnitude. Thus, it is safe to conclude that the statistical relationships among the variables in the model were very strong and that the structural models were more than adequately specified by the variables included. Also, the variability of the data differed only slightly from year to year.

Results: Effects of Federal R&D Expenditures

Table 3 contains standardized measures of the indirect, direct, and total causal effects of federal R&D expenditures on Ph.D. production for the three fields of science developed from path coefficients in

Figure 8. Structural Model of the Effects of Federal R&D Expenditures on Graduate Degree Production, for the Years 1975–1978 for Engineering ($N = 73$)

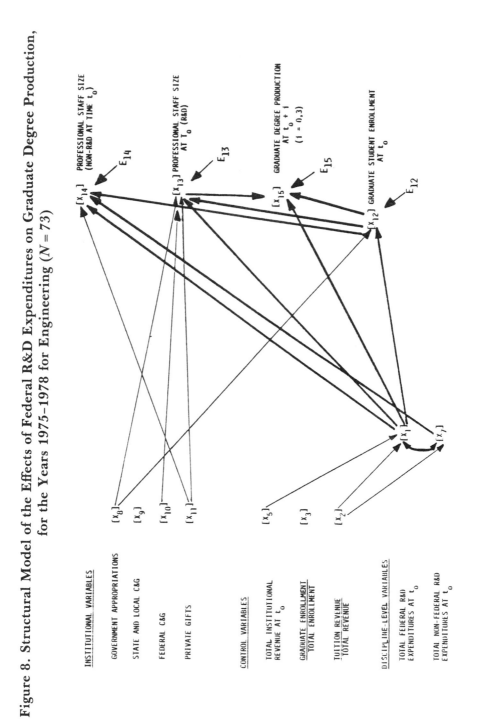

Table 3. Direct and Indirect Causal Effects Attributable to Federal R&D Expenditures in the Physical Sciences

Outcomes	Effects	Effect Coefficients				
		1975	*1976*	*1977*	*1978*	*1979*
Ph.D.'s conferred	Total	.59	.63	.62	.60	.56
	Direct	.18	.18	.23	.18	.12
	Indirect	.41	.45	.39	.42	.44

Direct and Indirect Causal Effects Attributable to Federal R&D Expenditures in the Biological Sciences

Outcomes	Effects	Effect Coefficients				
		1975	*1976*	*1977*	*1978*	*1979*
Ph.D.'s conferred	Total	.41	.54	.44	.50	.45
	Direct	.01	.16	.05	.25	.13
	Indirect	.40	.38	.39	.25	.32

Direct and Indirect Causal Effects Attributable to Federal R&D Expenditures in Engineering

Outcomes	Effects	Effect Coefficients				
		1975	*1976*	*1977*	*1978*	*1979*
Ph.D.'s conferred	Total	.67	.68	.63	.78	.84
	Direct	.33	.08	.43	.20	.00
	Indirect	.34	.60	.20	.58	.84

Note: Effects are measured by the number of standard deviations change in the outcomes attributable to a change of one standard deviation in federal R&D expenditures. In the first four columns, headcount data were used in the path analyses as measures of professional R&D staff size. In the last column, full-time-equivalent data were used.

the models presented in the preceding section. These measures are standardized effect coefficients. Each measures the number of standard deviations change in an outcome that results from a one standard deviation change in federal R&D expenditures, with the other variables being held constant. The effect coefficients are computed from the path coefficients of the structural models. For example, for engineering in 1978:

$$\text{Direct effect} = P_{15,1} = 0.20$$

$$\text{Indirect effect} = [(P_{15,12})(P_{12,1})] + [(P_{15,13})(P_{13,1})]$$
$$= [(0.84)(0.80)] + [(-0.11)(0.83)]$$

$$= 0.67 - 0.09$$
$$= 0.58$$

Total effect $= 0.20 + 0.58 = 0.78$

The data in Table 3 show clearly that the total effects of federal R&D expenditures on Ph.D. production remained relatively stable over the five-year period in all three fields of science. The greatest stability was in the physical sciences, and the least was in the biological sciences. Indirect effects were generally much greater than direct effects, and in the biological sciences the direct effects were very small or negligible. The greatest effects were observed in engineering, and the smallest effects were observed in the biological sciences. Other analyses indicated that in engineering the impact was greater on master's degree production than on Ph.D. production. Most of this impact was felt indirectly through graduate student enrollment and the strong linkage between graduate enrollment and master's degree production. In the other two fields, master's degree production was one of the smallest effects.

From these standardized effect coefficients and a knowledge of the standard deviations of the Ph.D. production and federal R&D expenditures variables, it was possible to quantify the effects in absolute terms. By *absolute*, we mean the actual number of Ph.D.s conferred in a given year that can be attributed to the influence of federal R&D expenditures. This is the "true" effect referred to by Macdonald (1977). Two indicators of effects were used: the influence of federal R&D expenditures on graduate degrees conferred as a percentage of the total size of these outcomes, and the net effect per $1 million of federal R&D expenditures.

Trends in the Effects on Ph.D. Production. Table 4 displays the contributions of federal R&D expenditures to the total number of Ph.D.s conferred each year. These contributions are expressed as percentage of the total number of Ph.D.s conferred that can be attributed to the total effects of federal R&D expenditures in the same year. The entries in the table are computed as follows:

$$\text{Percent} = \left[\frac{\Sigma X_1}{\Sigma X_{15}} \right] \left[\frac{\text{Standard deviation of } X_{15}}{\text{Standard deviation of } X_1} \right] \times 100$$

where $\Sigma X_1 =$ Total federal R&D expenditures

$\Sigma X_{15} =$ Total number of Ph.D.s conferred

Table 5 displays the absolute numbers of Ph.D.s attributable to the influence of each $1 million in federal R&D expenditures in the three

Table 4. Percentage of Ph.D.s Conferred Attributable to Federal R&D Expenditures

	Percent of Total Number of Ph.D.s Conferred Attributable to Federal R&D Expenditures					
Field of Science	1975 %	1976 %	1977 %	1978 %	1979 %	Mean %
Physical sciences	37	46	45	41	42	42
Biological sciences	36	49	38	32	38	42
Engineering	63	49	54	71	65	62

Note: Percentages have been rounded to the nearest whole number.

fields. Insufficient data points were available over time to allow statistical analysis of longitudinal trends, but the observation and inferences hold for the five-year window studied here.

Thus, in all three fields of science, for all five years studied, the influence of federal R&D expenditures on Ph.D. production was substantial. The data indicated that between 32 and 71 percent of the Ph.D.s conferred in any given year were influenced in some way by federal R&D expenditures in the same year. To a considerable extent, this impact was felt indirectly through the effects on full-time graduate enrollment.

The mechanisms by which R&D expenditures exercise influence

Table 5. Change in Number of Ph.D.s Conferred Attributable to Each $1 Million of Federal R&D Expenditures, Total Number of Degrees Conferred, and Total Federal R&D Expenditures

	Academic Year				
Field of Science	1975	1976	1977	1978	1979
Physical Sciences					
Change per $1 million	3.92	4.46	3.74	2.80	2.56
Total federal R&D expenditures[a]	188.19	202.43	226.15	161.07	302.20
Total number of degrees conferred	1,996.00	1,974.00	1,900.00	1,794.00	1,828.00
Biological sciences					
Change per $1 million	2.41	3.77	2.05	1.66	1.84
Total federal R&D expenditures[a]	297.98	336.49	366.30	387.82	432.59
Total number of degrees conferred	1,986.00	1,936.00	1,984.00	1,938.00	2,087.00
Engineering					
Change per $1 million	7.65	5.82	4.30	4.68	3.67
Total federal R&D expenditures[a]	150.25	169.46	192.55	224.09	264.77
Total number of degrees conferred	1,840.00	1,662.00	1,531.00	1,471.00	1,493.00

[a]In millions of dollars.

are not clear, nor was the study described here designed to reveal them. One obvious possibility, however, is that students completing dissertation work have been supported by graduate assistantships funded through sponsored research projects or by other more or less direct financial support that otherwise might not have been available. A less direct influence, perhaps, is the stimulus given to research activity by federal sponsorship, which in turn provides the climate, motivation, and opportunity to complete degree work, which might otherwise be deferred. At this point, causes are purely a matter of speculation, but the effect is apparent. Identifying the causes of the effects is worthy of research at the source — by institutions, faculty, and students.

The relative contribution of federal R&D expenditures to Ph.D. production remained relatively stable over the years at quite high levels. This stability was accompanied by steadily increasing levels of spending even after adjustment for inflation, so that the overall effects were sustained despite a decline in the effects per $1 million; however, greater levels of expenditures were needed in order to preserve them.

Federal R&D expenditures had their greatest influence on degree completion in engineering and their least influence in the biological sciences. However, federal R&D expenditures were lowest in engineering and highest in biological sciences. That trend was consistent over all five years of data. This finding suggests that biological sciences and engineering differed in the ways in which spending affected students and staff. It is possible, for example, that these differences actually represent differences in the costs of conducting research in the two fields. Also, the assumption that increased R&D expenditures means increased R&D activity may need to be interpreted within a curriculum area. It may well be that the relatively fewer dollars spent on engineering than on biological or physical sciences reflected a higher level of actual R&D activity. The trends in the numbers of professional staff involved in R&D work in these two fields tend to support that inference. The size of professional R&D staff in the biological sciences actually declined between 1976 and 1979, but in engineering there was a steady increase over the same period. In short, engineering research may be more labor-intensive than research in the biological sciences, and federal spending may therefore have a greater impact on students and staff.

Although the effects of total expenditures have remained at roughly the same levels because expenditures have increased, the effect of federal R&D dollars on Ph.D. production has declined in all three fields. This decline was particularly marked in engineering, where it fell to one half its value between 1975 and 1978 — from 7.65 Ph.D.s per million to 3.67 Ph.D.s per million.

Our first inclination was to attribute all this decline to the drop in the value of the dollar owing to inflation. However, the decline was still evident after adjustment for inflation. At the same time, Ph.D. production generally declined during the 1975–1978 period. Total graduate enrollment remained stable or increased slightly, and master's degree production either increased or remained at the same level. These findings suggest that graduate students are turning away from longer-term research degrees, such as the Ph.D., toward shorter-term training in preparation for entering the work force.

These suggestions are generally in line with what many institutions and specialists in academic science have observed, namely, that it is becoming increasingly difficult to attract and retain students in Ph.D. programs against the attractions of outside forces. A variety of reasons are offered: the deteriorating economic climate, the increasing cost of education, and a job environment that offers attractive short-term incentives. All these factors have created fierce competition for able scientists and engineers. In view of such competition, federal R&D expenditures appear to have played a very important role in helping institutions to compete for students against outside forces. Since the Ph.D. is principally the degree of the scholar and researcher, federal support to academic research can be said to have made an important contribution to the maintenance of an adequate research pool in academia. It is possible that Ph.D. production would have been further reduced without the federal R&D expenditures. If these trends continue into the future, more fueling of the academic research community may be needed in order to offset the competition from outside forces and to maintain an adequate research pool.

Differences Between Public and Private Institutions. The organization, governance structure, and operation of public and private universities differ in a number of respects that affect the manner in which they finance and conduct research and educate graduate students. There is reason to believe that these differences can influence the way in which federally sponsored research affects the production of graduate degrees. A series of analyses was performed to assess these differences.

Path-analytic models were constructed for the two groups of universities. From the path coefficients, standardized effects of federal R&D expenditures on outcomes were computed and compared. Sample sizes for both groups were quite small for regression analysis — forty-four for the public group and twenty-nine for the private group. However, the multiple correlations were reasonably high and comparable to those obtained with the full models. The large values of R^2

indicate that the fit between the data and the regression models was good. There were differences between the public and private models, and these differences were not the same in each field of science.

Physical Sciences. The strengths of the statistical relationships were quite strong for the physical sciences in both the public and private school models, as indicated by the high values of R^2, the percentage of explained variance in the variables. There were several key differences between the two models. In private universities, federal R&D expenditures had a direct impact on Ph.D. production, but in public universities they did not. Graduate student enrollment was very strongly linked to Ph.D. production in both public and private universities. Finally private gifts to the institution emerged as an influence on Ph.D. production in private universities but not in public universities. In general, federal contracts and grants were prominent in the private schools model, and state and local government appropriations were prominent in the public schools model as control variables.

Biological Sciences. In the biological sciences, the major differences between the public and private models was that federal R&D expenditures were linked to Ph.D. production only in private schools. Generally, the statistical relationships were weaker in the biological sciences than they were in the other two fields.

Engineering. In engineering, the public and private school models followed much the same pattern as they did for the physical sciences, except that linkages were generally stronger, and federal R&D expenditures had a small but significant effect on Ph.D. production in public schools. Thus, the single most striking finding of our analysis of differences between public and private institutions was that federal R&D expenditures had a considerably larger impact on Ph.D. production in private universities than they did in public universities in all three fields of science.

Conclusions

The study whose methods and results have been described in this chapter was directed toward five research questions. We repeat those questions here and summarize the results for each one. The full tabulations, analyses, and findings are presented in the final report on the study.

First, can path analysis produce a credible causal model to assess the impact of federally sponsored R&D on specified educational outcomes? In the physical sciences and engineering, the models were very stable over the 1975–1979 period. There was some question about the stability of the models when full-time-equivalent data were used as measures of professional staff size in 1978 and 1979. The models were well specified by the variables included in the models and the networks of linear regression relationships among them. The situation was somewhat different in the biological sciences. Although the models constructed for each year were adequately specified, there was some variation from year to year in both the variables that remained in the model and in the magnitudes of the path coefficients, and there was less consistency in the patterns of relationships among the variables than there was in physical sciences or engineering.

Second, are the models that are developed stable over time? The models for physical sciences and engineering showed considerable stability over time. The model for biological sciences tended to be less stable than the models for the other two fields of science, and it is not clear whether a single structural model can be constructed for this field. Of the three, the physical sciences model appears to be the most stable.

Third, do different models emerge for different fields of science? The models for physical sciences and engineering were very similar, and both differed from the models for biological sciences. Overall, the engineering models exhibited the strongest linkages among variables, but the physical sciences models showed the greatest stability over time both in the constancy of path coefficients and in the magnitude of effects on outcomes.

Fourth, do different models emerge for groups of public and private universities? Different models emerged for public and private universities, and overall there were some marked differences in the effects of federal spending in public and private universities. By far the greatest effect of federally sponsored R&D expenditures was observed in the private universities, and the differences between public and private universities were most apparent in the biological sciences.

Fifth, what are the measurable effects of federal R&D expenditures? Are they logical, and does informed opinion consider them to reflect reality? The most general conclusion one could draw from the results reported here was that federal R&D dollars had a considerable effect on Ph.D. production. Further, there were causal chains through which the effect was felt, in addition to direct linkages with R&D expenditures. The same effects were not apparent with nonfederal R&D expenditures.

While the effects of federal R&D dollars on Ph.D. production were maintained at substantial and relatively stable levels, this stability was an effect of increased spending levels. The actual strength of the relationship between R&D expenditures and Ph.D. production declined steadily in all fields over the 1975–1979 period, although there was some indication of a recovery in 1979. The steepest decline was observed in the biological sciences, although it was substantial in all disciplines. These declines were offset by increased expenditures which served to maintain the overall level of effect.

The largest effects were observed in engineering, and the smallest effects were observed in the biological sciences. This finding was directly contrary to the spending levels in those fields. One explanation may be that the costs of conducting research are different for these disciplines. There are, no doubt, other possibilities.

There is evidence that universities, particularly the major research institutions, are experiencing considerable difficulty in attracting and retaining graduate students against the competition from industry and business and that constraints on university growth are restricting faculty growth, particularly among new or young faculty. In view of this evidence, it can be said that the influence of federal support on academic research continues to be important for maintaining the viability of graduate education in science and engineering. Although this influence has been considerable, our analyses suggest that increasing levels of federal spending may be needed to maintain the levels of influence into the future. Moreover, federal expenditures may have to be specifically focused if they are to have the maximum effect on graduate student enrollments and degree production.

Finally, we return to the question of whether the use of secondary analysis of existing data bases is a useful alternative to a large scale original data collection effort. In this case, we feel that it is. Qualitatively, many of the findings are not surprising, or new, except in their quantitative aspect. But the fact that conventional wisdom tends to agree with the results of the statistical analyses lends credence to the quantitative findings and to the utility of the approach. Obviously, this will not always be the case. The intention is not to offer secondary analysis as a panacea for the headaches of data collection in evaluation and policy research. Rather, it is to recommend that researchers explore the data that already exist or are being collected elsewhere before undertaking an expensive data collection effort. There are a variety of analytical techniques and approaches available, such as the one used here, that can be applied to the analysis of such data. If researchers can learn to tap their potential, the analytical power implicit in these large sets of data is formidable.

APPENDIX A

Table A1. Standardized Path Coefficients for the Physical Sciences Model[a]

Variables			Path Coefficients (P_{ij})				
Outcomes (X_i)	Antecedent Variable (X_j)	P_{ij}	1975	1976	1977	1978	1979
Ph.D.s Conferred (X_{15})		R^{2b}	92%	94%	91%	92%	85%
	Federal R&D expenditures (X_1)	$P_{15,1}$	.12	.18	.23	.18	.12
	Graduate student enrollments (X_{12})	$P_{15,12}$	.73	.72	.70	.86	.82
Graduate Student Enrollment (X_{12})		R^{2b}	81%	79%	79%	76%	80%
	Federal R&D expenditures (X_1)	$P_{12,1}$	.56	.62	.56	.49	.54

[a] The standardized path coefficients are the numbers of standard deviation changes in the outcome (X_i) for one standard deviation change in the antecedent variable (X_j).

[b] R^2 is the percentage of the variance in Ph.D. production accounted for by variables in the model.

Table A2. Standardized Path Coefficients for the Biological Sciences Model[a]

Variables		Path Coefficients (P_{ij})					
Outcomes (X_i)	Antecedent Variable (X_j)	P_{ij}	1975	1976	1977	1978	1979
Ph.D.s Conferred (X_{15})		R^{2b}	83%	81%	85%	79%	80%
	Federal R&D expenditures (X_1)	$P_{15,1}$	–	.16	–	.25	.13
	Professional staff size (X_{13})	$P_{15,13}$	.16	–	.14	–	.22
	Graduate student enrollment (X_{12})	$P_{15,12}$	.70	.67	.70	.68	.51
Number of Professional Staff Primarily Engaged in R&D (X_{13})		R^{2b}	64%	60%	53%	59%	55%
	Federal R&D expenditures (X_1)	$P_{13,1}$	.24	.45	.48	.37	.76
	Graduate student enrollment (X_{12})	$P_{13,12}$	.35	–	–	–	–
	Nonfederal R&D expenditures (X_7)	$P_{13,7}$	.30	.15	.24	.32	.27
Total Graduate Student Enrollment (X_{12})		R^{2b}	69%	67%	74%	66%	73%
	Federal R&D expenditures (X_1)	$P_{14,1}$	.51	.48	.36	.37	.30

[a] The standardized path coefficients are the numbers of standard deviation changes in the outcome (X_i) for one standard deviation change in the antecedent variable (X_j).

[b] R^2 is the percentage of the variance in Ph.D. production accounted for by variables in the model.

Table A3. Standardized Path Coefficients for the Engineering Model[a]

Variables		Path Coefficients (P_{ij})					
Outcomes (X_i)	Antecedent Variable (X_j)	P_{ij}	1975	1976	1977	1978	1979
Ph.D.s Conferred (X_{15})		R^{2b}	96%	92%	95%	96%	97%
	Federal R&D expenditures (X_1)	$P_{15,1}$	.33	—	.43	.20	.13
	Graduate student enrollment (X_{12})	$P_{15,12}$	.45	.78	.56	.84	.89
	Professional staff size (X_{13})	$P_{15,13}$	.14	—	-.25	-.11	-.23
Number of Professional Staff Primarily Engaged in R&D (X_{13})		R^{2b}	93%	83%	73%	80%	79%
	Federal R&D expenditures (X_1)	$P_{13,1}$	1.21	1.02	1.15	.83	.57
	Graduate student enrollment (X_{12})	$P_{13,12}$	-.48	-.23	-.39	—	
Total Graduate Student Enrollment (X_{12})		R^{2b}	87%	79%	86%	84%	85%
	Federal R&D expenditures (X_1)	$P_{12,1}$	.70	.83	.87	.80	.81

[a] The standardized path coefficients are the numbers of standard deviation changes in the outcome (X_i) for one standard deviation change in the antecedent variable (X_j).

[b] R^2 is the percentage of the variance in Ph.D. production accounted for by variables in the model.

110

References

Alwin, D. F., and Hauser, R. M. "The Decomposition of Effects in Path Analysis." *American Sociological Review,* 1975, *40,* 37–47.

Blalock, H. M. *Causal Models in the Social Sciences.* Chicago: Aldine, 1971.

Bowering, D. J. *Research Study of the Direct and Indirect Effects of Federally-Sponsored R&D in Science and Engineering at Leading Research Institutions.* Washington, D.C.: National Science Foundation, 1981.

Duncan, O. D. *Introduction to Structural Equation Models.* New York: Academic Press, 1975.

Grodzins, L. "Prospects of Young Faculty in Physics and Other Science and Engineering Fields in 1990." In M. S. McPherson (Ed.), *The Demand for New Faculty in Science and Engineering.* Washington, D.C.: National Academy of Sciences, 1980.

Macdonald, K. I. "Path Analysis." In C. A. O'Murcheartaigh and C. Payne (Eds.), *The Analysis of Survey Data. Vol. 1: Model Fitting.* New York: Wiley, 1977.

Macdonald, K. I., and Doreian, P. *Regression and Path Analysis.* London: Methuen, 1977.

Teich, A. H., and Lambright, W. H. "The Consequences of Limited University Growth." In *National Science Foundation Annual Science and Technology Report to Congress.* Washington, D.C.: National Science Foundation, 1981.

Wolfle, L. M. "Strategies of Path-Analysis." *American Educational Research Journal,* 1980, *17,* 183–209.

David J. Bowering is vice-president in charge of the Management and Information Sciences Division at Science Management Corporation, Washington, D.C.

Index

111

S

St. John, E. P., 56, 72
Sample: describing status of, on selected populations, 31; projecting, to a universe, 31–32
Sample skews, in data file preparation, 36–37
Sample-verification techniques, 45–46
Schultz, L. J., 49
Seattle and Denver Income Maintenance Experiments, 21
Secondary analysis: compromises in, 23–24, 40; reasons for, 22–23, 27–28; steps in, 28
Securities and Exchange Commission, 7
Siegel, P., 21
Social Science Research Council, 14, 24
Social Security Administration, 7
Software packages: and data file preparation, 43; matching data bases with, 16–17
Sowell, E. J., 42, 49
Spiegelman, R., 21
SPSS, 16, 17, 30, 43, 82, 90
SRI International, 21
Statistical Analysis System (SAS), 16, 17, 30, 43, 46, 65–66
Steinbrenner, K., 49
Summary tape, as dissemination mode, 11, 12
Survey of Income and Education, 21
Survey of Income and Program Participation, 9, 21
Sustaining Effects Study of Title I, 21

T

Taeuber, R. C., 7, 14, 22, 25
Tatsuoka, M. M., 47, 49
Teich, A. H., 74, 110
Time tangles, in data file preparation, 38
Tingley, P., 72
Title III data base, 56
Torgerson, W., 47, 49
Tukey, J. W., 44, 49
Turner, C. F., 5, 25

U

United Nations, linkages with, 10
U.S. Bureau of Justice Statistics, 8–9, 10
U.S. Bureau of Labor Statistics, 8–9, 52, 53, 63, 65, 72
U.S. Bureau of the Census, 6, 8, 9, 13–14, 17, 21, 22, 23, 25, 30, 42, 51, 52, 53, 54, 56, 59, 63, 72; Data Users Services Division (DUSD) of, 10, 19
U.S. Department of Agriculture, 7, 8
U.S. Department of Commerce, 8
U.S. Department of Defense, Defense Manpower Data Center of, 7
U.S. Department of Education, 7
U.S. Department of Health and Human Services (HHS), 20
U.S. Department of Housing and Urban Development, 8
U.S. Department of Justice, 8
U.S. Department of Labor, 7, 8
U.S. National Archives and Records Service, 10, 14, 21, 25, 30
U.S. National Technical Information Service (NTIS), 10, 14, 25
Units of analysis and of organization, changing, in data file preparation, 33
User tapes. See Data bases

V

Van Alstyne, C., 52, 56, 72
Variable-construction techniques, 33–34, 47
Variant variables, in data file preparation, 37
Vocational Education Data Survey, 58

W

Waldenberg, A., 64, 72
Westat, 9, 22, 60, 72
Withers, J. S., 72
Wolanin, T. R., 55, 70
Wolfle, L. M., 78, 110
Wortman, P. M., 27, 28, 48

From the Editor's Notes

Perhaps the most costly and time-consuming aspect of evaluation and policy research is the data collection component. Large data collection efforts consume large amounts of resources — people, time, and money. At the heart of this volume of New Directions for Program Evaluation *is the proposition that there is an alternative that has been largely overlooked by researchers — the secondary analysis of extant data bases.*